THE MARTHA WASHINGTON COOK BOOK

by Marie Kimball

COWARD-McCANN

HERE is a fine cook book which is also rare and amusing Americana. Prepared from the original manuscript given by Frances Parke Custis to Martha Washington which has hitherto never been released for publication by The Historical Society of Pennsylvania, *The Martha Washington Cook Book* presents the "rules" which brought fame to America's first First lady as housewife and hostess throughout her life. The recipes have been completely modernized, and Mrs. Kimball offers in her Introduction a remarkably interesting and entertaining account of the Washingtons and their domestic problems. The book contains three reproductions in grafatone, including a frontispiece portrait of Martha Washington; three reproductions from the original manuscript; and numerous decorations in black and white; it is printed on water-resistant paper, and bound in washable cloth with lovely decorative endpapers.

Designed and Illustrated by Alanson B. Hewes

MARTHA WASHINGTON
from the famous portrait by
Gilbert Stuart

THE MARTHA WASHINGTON COOK BOOK

by Marie Kimball

Profusely Illustrated

New York City

COWARD-MCCANN

1940

Published by:

James Direct, Inc.

500 S. Prospect Ave.

Hartville, Ohio 44632

U.S.A.

This historic edition produced by
Murry Broach Productions

Originally printed in 1940 by: COWARD-MCCANN, INC.

ISBN: 978-1-62397-018-5

Printing 12 11 10 9

MANUFACTURED IN THE UNITED STATES OF AMERICA

ACKNOWLEDGMENT

This publication, for the first time, of Martha Washington's Cook Book is made by generous authorization of the Historical Society of Pennsylvania, owner of the manuscript, who also gave permission to reproduce three pages of the original manuscript. Some of the material of the introduction was published in the *Saturday Evening Post* and is included by courtesy of its editors. The photographs of the dining room and kitchen and the plan of the kitchen garden of Mount Vernon are reproduced by kind permission of the Mount Vernon Ladies' Association, and the Stuart portrait of Martha Washington by that of the Museum of Fine Arts, Boston.

CONTENTS

ILLUSTRATIONS

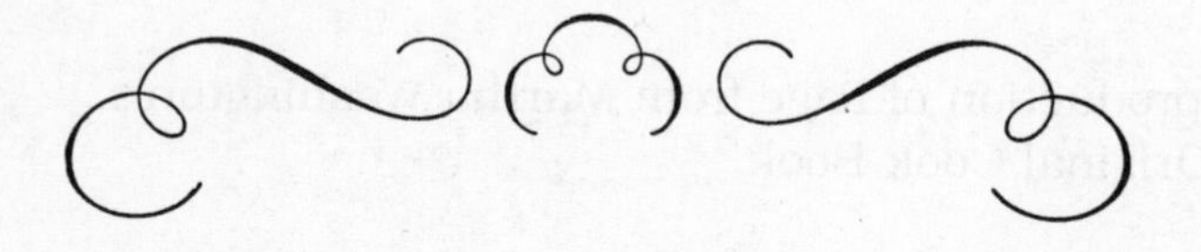

THE MISTRESS OF MOUNT VERNON

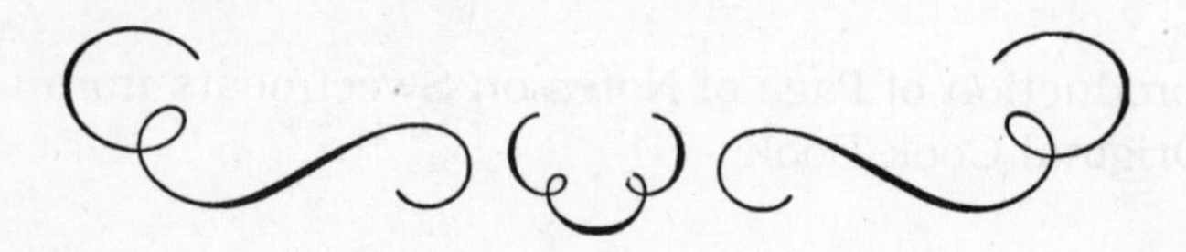

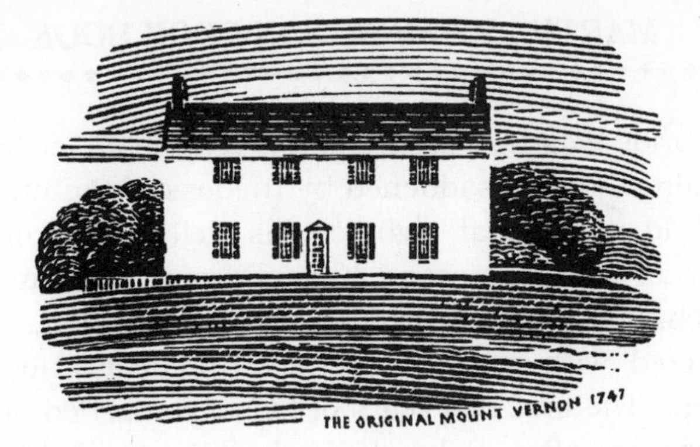

The MISTRESS *of* MOUNT VERNON

Early in the summer of 1759 Colonel George Washington of Virginia brought a new mistress to Mount Vernon, his plantation on the Potomac, not far from Alexandria. As all the world knows, she was the Widow Custis, born Martha Dandridge of New Kent County. She was young, handsome, and said to be the wealthiest widow in Virginia; yet so completely did she submerge her personality after this marriage that for decades she has seemed to lurk in the shadow of her famous husband, a vague and enigmatic figure. She has been described as an amiable but simple soul in a gray frock and a mobcap–a description to which Gilbert Stuart's portrait has lent some authenticity–interested chiefly in pots and pans and the routine of domestic life. Again, she has been pictured as the aloof and somewhat dressy "Lady Washington," wife of the President, whose Friday evening receptions were likely to take on much of the etiquette and dullness of a court function.

Of course, neither picture is true, and both are based on the woman the public came to know after George Washington had become the most celebrated man in his country. The young woman who came to Mount Vernon as a bride was but twenty-seven years old. Yet her life had already been saddened by the loss of the husband she had married at eighteen, as well as two of their children. On this second husband and her remaining two children she lavished an intense affection, always tempered with a tender yet fearful anxiety for their welfare. The first two years of her new married life was almost bucolic. Colonel Washington and his wife remained at Mount Vernon, except for the necessary visits to Williamsburg, where the Colonel was a member of the House of Burgesses. During this brief period Washington was able to indulge his passion for farming. "The life of a husbandman," he remarked, "of all others is the most delectable. It is honorable, it is amusing, and, with judicious management, it is profitable. To see plants rise from the earth and flourish by the superior skill and bounty of the laborer fills a contemplative mind with ideas which are more easy to be conceived than expressed."

The plantation was divided into five farms: Mansion House Farm, River Farm, Union Farm, Muddy Hole Farm, and Dogue Run Farm. It grew from an original two thousand five hundred acres to more than eight thousand, and offered Washington ample scope for his agricultural experiments.

To crowd his many activities into a day Washington rose with the sun, as he himself expressed it. "If my hirelings are not in their places by that time," he wrote, "I send them messages of sorrow for their indisposition; that, having put these wheels in motion, I examine the state of things further; that, by the time I have accomplished these matters, breakfast (a little after seven o'clock ...) is ready; that, this being over, I mount my horse and ride round my farm, which employs me till it is time to dress for dinner."

Martha Washington, who was naturally domestic in her tastes, had taken over the management of the Mansion. The duties of a Virginia housewife of this period were by no means nominal. Every small detail, from ordering the meals to directing the cooking and setting the table, was under her careful supervision; and Mrs. Washington took these duties very seriously. Thanks to her painstaking surveillance, there appeared upon the table at Mount Vernon many a fine repast that was the envy of her neighbors. As part of her dower she had brought one hundred fifty slaves. These, with those already on the estate, came under her particular care. Those not destined to become field hands had to be taught to spin and weave, to knit and sew, to cook and serve. All this the lady of Mount Vernon supervised and directed.

"She was remarkable for inspecting everything daily," one of her descendants writes, "giving out with her own hands the meals, going into dairy, cellar, etc. I have heard my mother say she always wore a white dimity dress on those occasions; that it was spotless and served her for a morning dress the whole week. Having well-trained servants, of course, it was not necessary that she should with her own hands perform any household duties."

Then there was the garden in which Mrs. Washington took particular interest. It was she who determined where the "pease" should be sown, in how many rows, and in what sheltered nook the herbs that distinguished the famous cuisine at Mount Vernon should be planted, how many "angelico stalks" should be rooted in April, and how many rosebuds would be needed for the "honey of roses" for which the Mistress of Mount Vernon was celebrated.

Life during these few busy and happy years was, of

course, not all work. The Washingtons joined in the gay, informal activities that have always characterized Virginia country life. There was the serious business of hunting the fox, always a favorite occupation with the Virginians, or shooting the duck in the near-by bays of the Potomac. Then there were visits back and forth to the neighboring plantations; there were dinners, tea parties, and hunt breakfasts, and once "the whole neighborhood was thrown into a paroxysm of festivity by the anchoring of the British frigate in the river, just in front of the hospitable mansion of the Fairfaxes. A succession of dinners and breakfasts takes place at Mount Vernon and Belvoir, with occasional tea parties on board the frigate."

There was never any lack of hospitality at Mount Vernon, either at this early period or later, when Washington was known throughout the land as the father of his country and when all the world, with a shadow of an excuse or without, poured into Mount Vernon until Washington was forced to complain that his home was "little better than a well-resorted inn." Indeed, so hospitable and generous were the Washingtons that, although a hundred cows grazed the fields of the plantation, they were not infrequently obliged to buy butter for the household. It was a characteristic order Washington left with the overseer of Mount Vernon when he went to take command of the American Army: "Let the hospitality of the house with respect to the poor be kept up. Let no one go hungry away. If any of this kind of people should be in want of corn, supply their necessaries, provided it does not encourage them to idleness; and I have no objection to your giving my money in charity to the amount of forty or fifty pounds a year where you think it well bestowed. What I mean by having no objection is, that it is my desire it should be done. You are to consider that neither myself nor wife, is now in the way to, do those good offices."

In May, 1775, George Washington journeyed to Philadelphia to attend the second Continental Congress, and in June he wrote his wife: "I now sit down to write to you on a subject that fills me with inexpressible concern, and this concern is greatly aggravated and increased when I reflect upon the uneasiness I know it will give you. It has been determined in Congress that the whole army raised for the defence of the American cause shall be put under my care, and that it is necessary for me to proceed immediately to Boston to take upon me the command of it." From this moment the peaceful and happy life at Mount Vernon came to an end, and it was not to be resumed until eight years later, when the victorious General returned to his home on Christmas Eve, 1783. During these eight years he was able to visit his plantation but twice once for only a single day, and Mrs. Washington divided her time between camp and Mount Vernon. A kinsman, Lund Washington, was left to run the estate. Domestic life was at a standstill.

With the return of the Washingtons to Mount Vernon, social life bloomed anew and to a degree never before known. George Washington was no longer merely a Virginia planter with a pleasant group of friends scattered over the neighboring country. From the moment of his arrival home he was not for one instant allowed to forget that he was a great public figure, and people flocked from the four corners of the earth to pay him respect or, as Washington realistically remarked, to look upon him with curiosity. Of that first Christmas Day we read: "I must tell you what a charming day I spent at Mount Vernon.... The Gen1 and Madame came home on Christmas Eve, and such a racket the servants made, for they were glad of their coming! Three handsome young Officers came with them. All Christmas afternoon people came to pay their Respects and Duty. Among them were stately Dames and gay young Women. The Genl seemed very happy and Mistress Washington was from Daybrake making everything as agreeable as possible for Everybody."

The guests continued to arrive at all seasons of the year and at all hours of the day, with little regard for the convenience of their host and hostess. Houdon, the famous French sculptor, who had been commissioned by Jefferson, then Minister to France, to execute a bust of Washington for the State of Virginia, arrived with three assistants at eleven o'clock one evening. The household had to be roused from sleep, rooms prepared, and a supper served to the weary Frenchmen, who doubtless felt they had journeyed to the very end of the world. The General and his wife, we suspect, began to be a little worried over this influx of visitors, for Washington remarked: "My manner of living is plain, and I do not mean to be put out by it. A glass of wine and a bit of mutton are always ready, and such as will be content to partake of them are always welcome. Those who expect more will be disappointed."

Washington may have thought of his manner of life as plain. Yet the hospitality so generously dispensed showed a rare thoughtfulness and consideration for the comfort of his guests. "Your apartment was your house," says the Marquis de Chastellex, after a visit to Mount Vernon, "the servants of the house were yours; and while every inducement was held out to bring you into the general society of the drawing room, or at the table, it rested with yourself to be served or not with everything in your own chamber."

It was inevitable that such hospitality should be abused. This was especially true during the eight long years of Washington's Presidency, when strangers came from far and near. At last Washington felt obliged to write his manager, *à propos* of the amount of wine consumed: "I am led to observe that it is not my intention that it should be given to everyone who may incline to make a convenience of the house, in traveling; or who may be induced to visit it from motives of curiosity.–There are but three descriptions of people to whom I think it ought to be given:–first my *particular* and intimate acquaintances, in case business should call them there, such for instance as Doctr Craik-2dly some of the most respectable foreigners who may, perchance, be in Alexandria or the federal city ... or, thirdly, to persons of some distinction [such as members of Congress, etc.] who may be traveling through the country from North to South, or from South to North.... Unless some caution of this sort governs, I should be run to an expense as improper as it would be considerable."

Mount Vernon as it stood at this time, on Washington's return from the war, was a house of modest proportions, ample for a family the size of the Washington household but totally inadequate for elaborate entertaining or for the many guests the Washingtons were now called upon to house. In the summer of 1784 alterations were begun, and the house assumed its present aspect. It was doubled in size; the portico, which we think of as so typically Mount Vernon, was added at this time, as was the large dining room, often called the banquet hall. This room witnessed the flowering of Martha Washington's abilities as housewife and hostess. Here were held that long succession of breakfasts and dinners for which she became famous.

The burden of housekeeping and incessant entertaining began to be more than Mrs. Washington could stand. Her ever-thoughtful husband was quick to observe this and decreed that a housekeeper would have to be engaged. He wrote to Samuel Fraunces, in New York, asking for a reliable steward who could be "recommended for honesty, sobriety and knowledge of their profession, which is in a word to relieve Mrs. Washington of the drudgery of seeing the table properly covered and things economically used." A certain Mrs. Forbes was found for the place, and Mrs. Washington, freed from the petty details, was now able to devote herself to her guests, her two grandchildren, whom she and the General had adopted, and to overseeing the establishment in a general way.

In spite of these changes and in spite of the influx of visitors, life at Mount Vernon proceeded with much of its accustomed simplicity. Breakfast was still served at seven o'clock in the morning. Washington is said to have partaken only of hoe cakes, honey, and tea, but he did not expect his guests to be so modest. On the table was set the generous Southern breakfast that persists to this day: thin, crisp breakfast bacon, or fried ham, with scrambled eggs, corn cakes with plenty of butter and honey, and, of course, tea and coffee, although Washington considered coffee too expensive for daily use. Sometimes there were fried apples, and often there was fresh fish, turned a golden brown. An English visitor tells us that Mrs. Washington herself made the coffee and tea at table. One servant, without livery, waited on the table. "A silver urn for hot water was the only expensive piece of table furniture," our commentator concludes. Another guest tells of a breakfast "where a table was elegantly spread with ham, cold corn beef, cold fowl, red herring and cold mutton, the dishes ornamented with sprigs of parsley and other vegetables from the garden. At the head of the table was the tea and coffee equipage, where she [Mrs. Washington] seated herself, and sent the tea and coffee to the company.

Dinner at Mount Vernon was served at three o'clock and was a fairly formal meal. The General, who had been riding over the plantation dressed, we are told, "in a plain tan coat, white cassimir waistcoat and black breeches and Boots," came home in time to change "his clothes and put on the attire considered suitable to the occasion, his hair neatly powdered, a clean shirt on, a plain drab coat, white waistcoat and white silk stockings." Mrs. Washington and the guests likewise changed from their morning frocks. At table, "where everything was set off with a peculiar taste and at the same time very neat and plain," Mrs. Washington took her place at the head, with the General at her side to the left.

The dinners called forth the skill of the cook, whom Mrs. Washington had carefully trained. It was a time when heavy food and plenty of it was in vogue. A meal with four or five kinds of meat, fish, poultry, and several "made dishes" was not considered elaborate; it was expected. The many visitors who came to Mount Vernon stressed the excellence of the table as well as the unexpected informality. Brissot de Warville, a Frenchman who visited Washington at Mount Vernon at this time, says: "Everything has an air of simplicity in his house; his table is good, but not ostentatious; and no deviation is seen from regular and domestic economy. Mrs. Washington superintends the whole, and joins to the qualities of an excellent housewife, that simple dignity which ought to characterize a woman whose husband has acted the greatest part on the theatre of human affairs; while she possesses that amenity, and manifests that attention to strangers, which renders hospitality so charming." Another guest comments: "His table is always furnished with elegance and exuberance but it is devoid of Pomp; and whether he has company or not, he remains an hour at table in familiar conversation. It was the pleasant custom at Mount Vernon that each guest should drink a toast to some absent friend, and thus the hour passed agreeably and quickly."

The second idyllic period at Mount Vernon was destined to last but little longer than the first. In April, 1789, Washington was elected President of the United States of America, and the congenial life of country gentleman and farmer once more came to an end. Washington did not hesitate to say how loath he was to relinquish this life when he wrote his old friend General Knox: "My movements to the chair of government will be accompanied by feelings not unlike those of a culprit, who is going to the place of his execution; so unwilling am 1, in the evening of a life nearly consumed in public cares, to quit a peaceful abode for an ocean of difficulties."

For Mrs. Washington, with her home-loving nature and domestic inclinations, the break was even more difficult. She was fifty-eight years old. She had heroically left home and followed the General during the eight long years of war. Now she was once more called upon to relinquish so much that she loved. "Taught by the great example which I have so long before me never to oppose my private wishes to the public will," she could but acquiesce. It was only human that she should write: "I had little thought when the war was finished that any circumstances could possibly happen which would call the General into public life again. I had anticipated that, from that moment, we should be suffered to grow old together, in solitude and tranquility. That was the first and dearest wish of my heart. I will not, however, contemplate with too much regret disappointments that were inevitable; though his feelings and mine were in perfect unison with respect to our predilections for private life, yet I cannot blame him for having acted according to his ideas of duty in obeying the voice of his Country."

It took time to make the necessary arrangements for leaving Mount Vernon, and Mrs. Washington did not arrive in New York, then the capital, until May, 1789. A new life was to begin for her. The President had taken one of the finest houses in the city and had it in readiness. The elegance and luxury of the furnishings soon led it to be known as "The Palace." Some of the furniture belonged to the Washingtons; some was purchased by the Government. There was a "green Drawing Room," with sofa and chairs covered in flowered green damask and green silk curtains at the windows. The front drawing room was adorned with yellow damask, three yellow silk sofas, and ten yellow damask chairs. The large dining room, used for public occasions, was hung with crimson satin, and the small one, which the family used every day, with blue damask. With a wealth of inlaid and carved mahogany furniture, mirrors, lusters, girandoles, prints, and pictures, it was one of the handsomest establishments in the United States.

The most important question facing the Washingtons was that of etiquette. Hitherto, of course, the country had been ruled by royal governors, and there were no precedents. How the President should be addressed and how much ceremony should surround his household, his dinners and receptions, were burning questions. Should he be called "His Highness" or "His Excellency"? Should his wife be addressed as "Lady" Washington, as she often had been, or merely as "Mrs."? Washington, with his enormous store of common sense, gave much thought to these problems and determined many of the forms of social as well as political etiquette which have persisted to this day. Simplicity and decorum were stressed with only the amount of ceremony necessary to preserve the dignity of the office.

It was determined that Washington should hold a levee every Tuesday afternoon from three until four o'clock, when he would receive the foreign ambassadors and strangers of importance, and that Mrs. Washington's drawing-room would take place on Friday evenings. In addition, there were the Congressional dinners on Thursday nights and the usual State banquets. The levees seem to have been rather frigid and formal affairs. The guests, usually awe-struck, stood in a circle about the dining room, from which all seats had been removed. Washington entered, dressed in a "black velvet coat and breeches, his hair in full dress, powdered and gathered behind in a silk bag; yellow gloves and holding a cocked hat with a cockade on it, and the edge adorned with a black feather about an inch deep. He wore knee and shoe buckles, and a long sword with a finely wrought and polished steel hilt; the coat worn over the blade, the scabbard of polished leather." Washington, we are told by one of his visitors, "always stood in front of the fire place, with his face toward the door of entrance.... He received his visitor with a dignified bow, while his hands were so disposed of as to indicate that the salutation was not to be accompanied with shaking hands. This ceremony never occurred in these visits, even to his most near friends, that no distinction might be made. At a quarter past three the door was closed, and the circle was formed for that day. He then began on the right, and spoke to each visitor calling him by name, and exchanging a few words with him. When he had completed his circuit, he resumed his first position, and the visitors approached him in succession, bowed and retired. By four o'clock the ceremony was over."

Mrs. Washington's Friday evenings were rather less formidable. The company gathered about seven o'clock. Dressed in a handsome gown of satin or velvet, as the case might be, Mrs. Washington received her guests alone, while her husband, in a colored coat and waistcoat, with black breeches, but without hat or sword, mingled among the guests as one of them. The society of ladies was very agreeable to him, and he found no difficulty in passing about the circle exchanging pleasantries. Tea, coffee, and plum cake were passed, and at nine o'clock Mrs. Washington rose to withdraw. Charlotte Chambers, who was present at one of these evenings in 1795, has left a girlish and enthusiastic picture. After describing her own dress of white brocade, with light-blue sash and all the other details so important to a young woman on an occasion such as this, she observes: "The hall, stairs and drawing room of the President's house were well lighted by lamps and chandeliers. Mrs. Washington with Mrs. Knox sat near the fire place. Other ladies were seated on sofas, and gentlemen stood in the centre of the room conversing. On our approach Mrs. Washington rose and made a courtesy-the gentlemen bowed most profoundly-and I calculated my declension to her own with critical exactness. The President, soon after, with that benignity peculiarly his own, advanced, and I arose to receive and return his compliments with the respect and love my heart dictated."

The dinner parties which Mrs. Washington gave during her husband's Presidency and which so

The Dining Room at Mount Vernon

enhanced her reputation as a hostess, were held every Thursday at four o'clock. About the long dining table, with its handsome cloth, lavish silver, and the *surtout de table* which Gouverneur Morris had selected for Washington in Paris were gathered "as many as my table can hold." The accounts of these parties may differ with the political complexion of the commentator, but all contemporaries agree that "Washington's dinner parties were entertained in a very handsome style." A member of Congress from Massachusetts gives us a vivid picture of one such occasion:

"Last Thursday I had the honor of dining with the President, in company with the Vice-President, the senators and Delegates of Massachusetts, and some other members of Congress, about twenty in all. In the middle of the table was placed a piece of table furniture about six feet long and two feet wide rounded at the ends. It was either of wood gilded, or polished metal, raised only about an inch, with a silver rim round it like that round a tea board; in the centre was a pedestal of plaster of Paris with images upon it, and on each end figures, male and female of the same. It was very elegant and used for ornament only. The dishes were placed all around and there was an elegant variety of roast beef, veal, turkey, ducks, fowls, hams, etc.; puddings, jellies, oranges, apples, nuts, almonds, figs, raisins, and a variety of wines and punch. We took our leave at six, more than an hour after the candles were introduced. No lady but Mrs. Washington dined with us. We were waited on by four or five men servants, dressed in livery."

William Maclay, the Senator from Pennsylvania, grudgingly admits, on one occasion, that "it was a great dinner-all in the tastes of high life. I considered it as a part of my duty as a Senator to submit to it, and am glad it is over. The President is a cold, formal man; but I must declare that he treated me with great attention. I was the first person with whom he drank a glass of wine. The President and Mrs. Washington sat opposite each other in the middle of the table; the two secretaries, one at each end. It was a great dinner, and the best of the kind I ever was at. The room, however, was disagreeably hot. First the soup; fish roasted and boiled; meats, sammon, fowls, etc.... The middle of the table was garnished in the usual tasty way, with small images, flowers (artificial), etc. The dessert was apple pies, puddings, etc.; then iced creams, jellies, etc.; then water melons, musk-melons, apples, peaches, nuts. It was the most solemn dinner I ever was at. Not a health drank; scarce a word was said until the cloth was taken away. Then the President, filling a glass of wine, with great formality, drank to the health of every individual by name round the table. Everybody imitated him, changed glasses, and such a buzz of 'health, Sir,' and 'health, Madam,' and 'thank you, Sir,' and 'thank you, Madam,' never had I heard before.... The ladies sat a good while, and the bottles passed about; but there was a dead silence, almost. Mrs. Washington at last withdrew with the ladies. I expected the men would now begin, but the same stillness remained."

During the Presidency, the Washington household was presided over by a steward. Some of his duties are outlined in a letter Washington wrote to one Germain, in 1794. "In the first place I am to inform you, that all the liquors-the groceries-and other shop articles of consequence, will be laid in by my secretary. Trifling articles, which are only wanted occasionally, will be provided by yourself.... From Mr. Dandridge you will obtain the money to defray my expenses, and accounts weekly.... Ready money is to be paid for everything you purchase. I want no credit and am averse to after-reckonings. The multiplicity of my public duties leaves me but little leisure to suggest domestic arrangements.... For this reason I require that you would advise with Mrs. Washington on the several points and be governed by her directions. My general ideas on this subject are shortly these: 1st. that my table be handsomely but not extravagantly furnished on the days that company are entertained. 2nd. that a decent and economical board be spread at other times.... As we never have suppers nor sudden calls for extra dinners; it should not be a difficult matter to ascertain with certainty to what any expences (agreeably to the prevailing mode of living) may be reduced.... In consequence of your performing these services-and in full expectation of your paying particular attention to the cookery seeing that everything appertaining to it is conducted in a handsome style, but without waste or extravagance I agree to allow you fifty guineas a year...."

The first man to hold the post of steward was Samuel Fraunces formerly an innkeeper. Indeed, it was at Fraunces Tavern on Broad Street that Washington, on the conclusion of the war, had said farewell to his officers in 1783. Fraunces was a man of great ability, he not only performed the duties of the present-day butler but was, as Washington observed, "an excellent cook, knowing how to provide genteel dinners, and giving aid in dressing them, prepared the dessert, made the cake, etc." Unfortunately, Fraunces was a man of very extravagant tastes. He was determined that the President's table should be "bountiful and elegant," and he was equally determined that the second table should be the same. Washington remonstrated frequently, but his remarks fell upon deaf ears.

During Fraunces' regime the cook had been one Mrs. Read. Between them they seem to have kept open house below stairs. Sorely tried, Washington dismissed Mrs. Read after eight months' service and subsequently the invaluable Fraunces. Mrs. Read seems to have outraged him particularly. When Fraunces was re-engaged in May, 1791, he tried to have Mrs. Read reinstated. Washington wrote: "This idea would be well for him to relinquish at once and forever; for unless there are reasons inducing it, which my imagination cannot furnish, it will never happen. Hercules can answer every purpose that Mrs. Read would do and others which she will not...."

With the dismissal of Mrs. Read, the eternal cook problem loomed very large in the Washington household. At Mount Vernon it had been simple; there was Hercules, the genial old chief cook, and his son, Richmond, who acted as assistant. When Washington assumed the Presidency, he determined to employ white servants, with a few trusted and indispensable slaves brought from Virginia. The winter of 1789 found him advertising in the papers for a cook for the "family of the President of the United States."

A Cook

Is wanted for the family of the President of the United States. No one need apply who is not perfect in the business, and can bring indubitable testimonials of sobriety, honesty and attention to the duties of the station.

A satisfactory person was not immediately forthcoming, and the advertisement continued for more than two months. Meanwhile Rachel Lewis, one of the kitchen maids, took charge of the cooking. She seems to have made quite as bad an impression as Mrs. Read, if for a different reason. On the removal to Philadelphia, Washington wrote his secretary: "In my last I left it to you to decide on the propriety of bringing the washerwomen and I do so still. But with respect to Mrs. Lewis and her daughter, I wish it may not be done, especially as it is in contemplation to transport Hercules and Nathan from the kitchen at Mount Vernon to that here in Philadelphia; and because the dirty figures of Mrs. Lewis and her daughter will not be a pleasant sight in view (as the kitchen always will be) of the principal entertaining rooms of our new habitation."

Mrs. Lewis' attempts at cooking lasted only a brief time. She was succeeded by a Frenchman named Lamuir who remained a month. Finally a chef was obtained from Baltimore, by the name of John Vicar, and the domestic difficulties were over for the time being.

Vicar, unfortunately, was not able to make cake, and the Washingtons were obliged to buy the cakes served at the drawing rooms and dinner parties during this period, something Mrs. Washington much resented.

On Fraunces' dismissal as steward, a certain Mr. Hyde was engaged to fill his place, and as Mr. Hyde was unable to make the desserts and cakes, Mrs. Hyde was employed for that purpose. It was not long before the Hydes were attacked by the same disease to which Fraunces had succumbed-extravagance. Washington urged his secretary to compare the accounts of the two men and added: "I strongly suspect that *nothing* is brought to my table of liquors, fruits, or other things that is not used as *profusely* at his." After much discussion, Hyde and his wife went with the household to Philadelphia, but they lasted only a few months. Hyde was dismissed early in 1791, and Vicar took his place until a new steward could be found. As usual, an advertisement appeared in the papers, but in the end Fraunces was reengaged. Washington wrote his secretary: "Who the steward and housekeeper shall be, must be left to Mrs. Washington and yourself to determine. Fraunces.... I should prefer for reasons already mentioned to you-but be him or them who they may, it must be expressly understood that wine is not admissible at their table.... If Fraunces is employed, it ought to be made known to him that his services in the kitchen as usual will be expected, and that in case of the present cook's leaving me or attempting to raise his wages; that he is to do with Hercules and such under aids as shall be found indispensably necessary...." In May, 1791, Vicar was discharged. Fraunces returned and a Mrs. Emerson was engaged as housekeeper. Both were to remain with the Washington household until the final return to Mount Vernon in 1797.

In November, 1790, Hercules, the cook at Mount Vernon, was brought to Philadelphia, along with Austin, Richmond, and Christopher. "The former," Washington observed, "(not for his appearance or merits I fear-but because he was the son of Hercules and his desire to have him as an assistant) comes as a scullion for the kitchen." Hercules lived up to his name in physique. He was as enchanted by city life as little Nellie Custis, who spent hours staring out of the windows. Hercules, however, turned into a dandy and spent the evenings parading the streets of darktown, drinking in admiration. His city days, however, were to be intermittent. There was a law in Pennsylvania giving slaves their freedom after six months' residence. Although Washington did not believe Hercules would avail himself of this, it was considered prudent to return him to Mount Vernon before the six months were up. Henceforth Hercules shuttled back and forth between Mount Vernon at intervals. In the end, city life got the better of him. When the family was to return home, in 1797, Hercules ran away and was never seen again.

During the Presidency, fifteen white servants were employed in the household. The house maids, kitchen maids, and washerwomen received four dollars a month; but when the capital was moved to Philadelphia, such a shortage of servants developed that it was necessary to raise the wages to five dollars. The steward received the handsome sum of twenty-five dollars. There were also from five to seven slaves in the establishment. Cabals below stairs were as frequent there as now, and all seem to have come to the President's attention. His faithful secretary, Tobias Lear, acted as a super major-domo, and in letters to him Washington warns that the white servants must be prevented from conspiring against the black, against

The Kitchen at Mount Vernon

the housekeeper, or against the steward. When at Mount Vernon, in June, 1791, Washington saw fit to write his secretary in Philadelphia: "It might not be improper to hint to the Servants who are with you (before they are joined by those with me) that it will be very idle and foolish in them to enter into any combination for the purpose of supplanting those who are now in authority; for the attempt, in the first place, will be futile and must recoil upon themselves; and because admitting they were to make the lives of the present steward and housekeeper, so uneasy as to induce them to quit, others would be got to supply their places; and such, too, as would be equally, if not more rigid, in the exaction of the duties required of the servants. In a word, that these Characters are indispensably necessary to take trouble off the hands of Mrs. Washington and myself and will be supported.... A good and faithful servant is never afraid or unwilling to have his conduct looked into."

When the Washingtons returned to Mount Vernon at the conclusion of his Presidency, the free and simple hospitality of the early days was resumed. Washington tried once more to be an unassuming farmer, and as such he conducted himself, riding over his plantation in the morning as he had done so many years before. When he returned for dinner, it was always to find one or more of the curious public ready to join him at his board. "The President came and desired us," one visitor writes, "to walk into dinner and directed us where to sit. (No grace was said).... The dinner was very good, a small roasted pigg, boiled leg of lamb, roasted fowles, beef, pease, lettice, cucumbers, artichokes, etc. puddings, tarts, etc. etc. We were desired to call for what drink we chose...."

From another guest we learn that, "at three, dinner was on the table, and we were shown by the General into another room, where everything was set off with a peculiar taste and at the same time neat and plain. The General sent the bottle about pretty freely after dinner. . . . After Tea General Washington retired to his study and left us with the ... rest of the Company.... We had a very elegant supper about that time (nine o'clock). The General with a few glasses of Champagne got quite merry, and being with his intimate friends laughed and talked a great deal. Before strangers he is very reserved, and seldom says a word.... At twelve I had the honor of being lighted up to my bedroom by the General himself."

THE COOK BOOK

THE KITCHEN BUILDING, MOUNT VERNON

THE COOK BOOK

In the Division of Manuscripts of the Historical Society of Pennsylvania lies a small, brown, leather-bound book. It is the cook book used at Mount Vernon, the "rules" from which brought fame to Martha Washington as housewife and hostess. She did not compile the book; nor did she copy the rules. As an inscription testifies, the book was written by Frances Parke Custis, the mother of Martha Washington's first husband. She gave it to her daughter-in-law, and Martha Washington, in turn, toward the end of her life, bestowed it upon her adored granddaughter, Nelly Custis, after her marriage to Lawrence Lewis. The inscription reads:

> "This book, written by Eleanor Parke Custis's great grand-mother Mrs. John Custis, was given to her, by her Beloved Grandmamma Martha Washington–formerly Mrs. Daniel Custis."

The volume is divided into "A Booke of Cookery," containing two hundred and five recipes, and "A Booke of

Sweetmeats," with three hundred and twenty-six. The pages are written in black ink, in a bold angular hand, and the spelling calls sharply to mind that Frances Parke, who was married in 1706, had learned her reading and writing in the late seventeenth century. At that time one was taught how to make a "frykasie," to "stew a neck of muton with orringes," to "roule a coller of beefe," or to make "a pease porrage of old pease." There were "hartychoakes," "mushrumps," "sparragus," "a tarte of lettice," and even "a tarte of Hipps," which is not what one might be tempted to think it is. Indeed, Mrs. John Custis is very reminiscent in spelling, as well as in the character and names of the recipes, of E. Smith's *The Compleat Housewife* or Mrs. Glasse's *Art of Cookery*, two eighteenth-century household stand-bys printed originally in London but much used in the colonies. There is nothing about the cook book to distinguish it as being typically American, no reference to scrapple, sweet potatoes, spoon bread, or the many other victuals and viands that are so typically our own. On the contrary, with the famous "Dr. Stephens, his cordiall water," Lady Amitage's cordiall water, and Lord Verney's Usquebath" it has a distinctly English flavor.

In reading over Martha Washington's cook book, we must bear in mind that the taste in cookery in the eighteenth century was very different from what it is today. It might be called as florid as the costumes of the period. Highly seasoned and spiced foods, meats cooked in wine with nutmeg and ginger; puddings, cakes, and creams with the lingering perfume of orange or rosewater were greatly prized. Condiments which have become rare, if not obsolete, in the cookery of the present and which, at best, may now be found only on the shelves of an apothecary were in daily use. Lemon and orange were favorite flavorings, but vanilla was

This Book, written by Eleanor Parke
Custis's Great GrandMother
Mrs John Custis, was given
to her, by her Beloved GrandMama
Martha Washington — formerly
Mrs Daniel Custis.

unknown to Martha Washington. It was introduced to America by Thomas Jefferson after his return from France in 1789.

It is significant that today we are gradually rediscovering the delicate and elusive flavors seemingly lost in the nineteenth century, and singularly lacking in the marshmallow, cream-cheese, maraschino-cherry school which has dominated American cooking for so many years. Herb farms and herb shops have sprung up all over the country. Again we are learning to appreciate the wistful flavor of rosemary, the tang of thyme or dried mint, coriander, anise, chervil, sorrel, basil, marjoram, balm, savory, eschalot, and tarragon.

There were, of course, certain dishes in which the combination of materials, spices, and flavors seems to us somewhat bizarre and inharmonious. It is a little difficult to imagine eating with any pleasure "white hogs' pudding," a sort of sausage, in which the skins had been thoroughly soaked in rosewater and the sausage meat mixed with almonds, currants, spices, sugar, and orangeflower water. Another curious concoction was a Florentine, esteemed a great delicacy. To make it, "take the kidney of a Loin of Veal, or the Wing of a Capon, or the leg of a Rabbit, mince any of these small with the kidney of a Loin of a Mutoon, if it be not fat enough. Then season it with cloves, mace, nutmeg, sugar, cream, currans, eggs and Rose-water; mingle these four together, and put them in a dish between two sheets of paste, then close it and cut the paste round by the brim of the dish; then cut it roundabout like Virginal keys, turn up one and let the other lye; pinch it, bake it, scrape sugar on it and serve it."

It must not be supposed, however, that the cooking at Mount Vernon was one long feast of Florentines, neats' tongues, and ears *variées*. And it is doubtless no more surprising that the ideas of a delicacy at that time should have been what they were than that we should esteem white caviar and sweetbreads, to say nothing of the meat of rattlesnakes. These things did not compose the main part of a dinner then, any more than ours do now. They were delicacies provided for a special

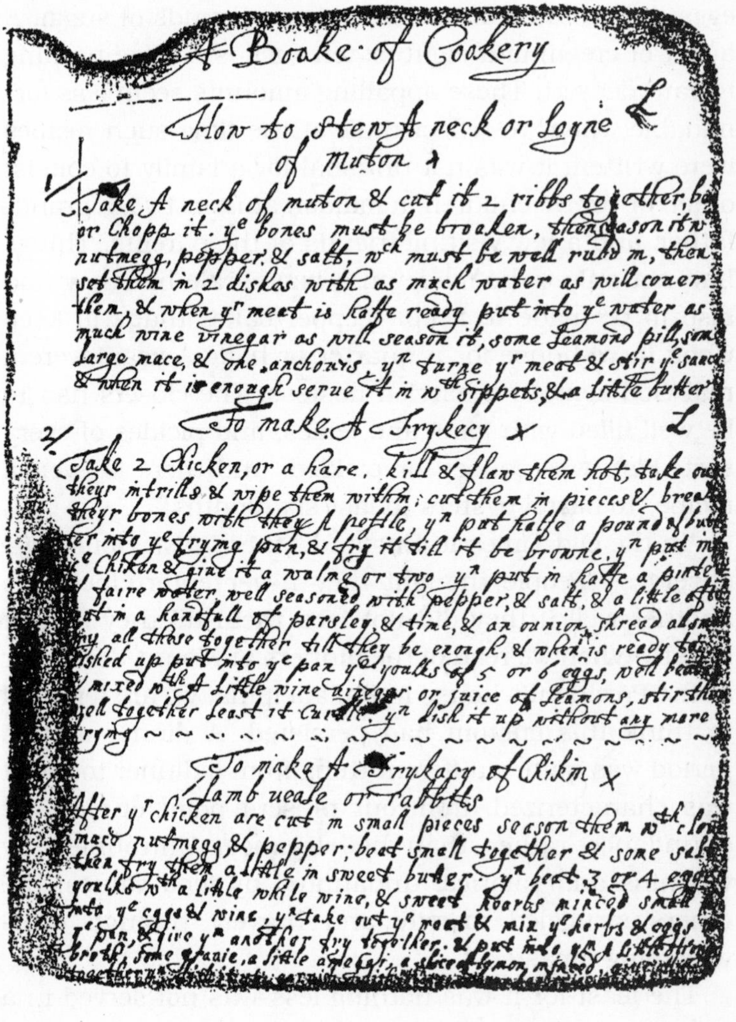

A Booke of Cookery

How to stew A neck or Loyne of muton L

1/ Take A neck of muton & cut it 2 ribbs together, be[at] or Chopp it. ye bones must be broaken, then season it w[ith] nutmegg, pepper & salt, wch must be well rubd in, then set them in 2 dishes with as much water as will cover them, & when yr meat is halfe ready put into ye water as much wine vinegar as will season it, some Leamond pill, som[e] large mace, & one anchovis, yn turne yr meat & stir ye sauce & when it is enough serve it in wth sippets, & a little butter

To make A Frykecy x L

2/ Take 2 Chicken, or a hare, kill & flaw them hot, take out theyr intrills & wipe them within; cut them in pieces & breake theyr bones with they A pestle, yn put halfe a pound of butter into ye frying pan, & fry it till it be browne, yn put in ye Chiken & give it a walme or two. yn put in halfe a pinte of faire water well seasoned with pepper, & salt, & a little after put in a handfull of parsley & time, & an ounion shreed along fry all these together till they be enough, & when is ready to be dished up put into ye pan ye youlks of 5 or 6 eggs, well beaten & mixed wth A little wine vinegar or juice of Leamons, stir them all together least it Curdle. yn dish it up without any more frying ~ ~ ~ ~ ~

To make A Frykacy of Chikin lamb veale or rabbits x

After yr chicken are cut in small pieces season them wth clove mace nutmegg & pepper; beat small together & some salt then fry them a little in sweet butter. yn beat 3 or 4 eggs youlks wth a little white wine, & sweet hearbs minced small into ye eggs & wine, yn take out ye meat & mix ye herbs & eggs [in] ye pan, & give yn another fry together. & put into yn A little strong broth, some gravie, a little anchovis, a slice of lymon, minced [illegible] together [illegible]

occasion, “pretty little Dishes for a supper, and little corner-dishes for a Great Table.”

As is the case in all old cook books, the quantities mentioned in the rules of the Washington cook book are enormous. For French bread you are directed to start with a gallon of flour. A rich black cake calls for twenty eggs, two pounds of butter, and two pounds of sugar. A quart of cream and eight or ten eggs is a mere nothing toward dessert. These appalling amounts seem less formidable when we reflect that, at the time such recipes were written, it was not unusual for a family to consist of ten or twelve children, a maiden aunt or two, a grandfather, and a few visiting friends of the parents. Things had not only to be made on a large scale but they had also to be made to keep. "Pepper cakes that will keep Good in ye house for A quarter or halfe A year" were a real God-send to a harried hostess. The closets had to be well filled with jams and jellies, and pickles of every sort. Fish was soused or pickled, and there is even a recipe "to barrel oysters to last six months."

"In the Old Times in England," the *British Housewife* observes, "People thought they never entertained one another well if they did not feed them till they almost burst." When we read of the dinners at Mount Vernon or at the President's house in Philadelphia, we are tempted to think this custom had persisted. A dinner at this period was quite a different thing from a dinner today. It was characterized, from our present point of view, by abundance rather than by elegance. Untroubled by vitamins and calories, undaunted by food values, the diners struggled merrily and bravely through overwhelming repasts.

The feast-for it was nothing less-was not served in a long series of courses but in two, which very thoroughly duplicated each other. Every dish for each course was put on the table at the same time, the hot dishes under covers. The table stretched nearly the full length of the room and was covered by a cloth-diaper cloth for every day, a more imposing material for festive occasions. The symmetrical arrangement of the dishes on the table was

A Booke of Sweetmeats

1 To know how to Clarefie your Sugar x

Take a pinte of faire water & beat ye white of an egg into it, to a froth, then put a pound of sugar in to it. & let it boyle uery fast. & there will rise a black scum on ye top of it, as it riseth take it of till it is uery clean, & then streyne it through A Jelly bagg or wet cloth. & soe use it as you please to euery pound of sugar as you clarefie, you must put a pinte of faire water, & ye white of an egg. ye white of one egge will clarefy 2 pound of sugar as well as one pound

2 To know when Sirrup is thin, or that your sugar is brought to a thin Surrup x.

After you have clarefied yr sugar, set it to boyle againe, & as there did rise a black scum in ye clarefying, soe there will rise another scum which will be white, wch you must take of uery clean as it riseth & when there will rise noe more, it is in a thinn sirrup, & it will look thin & pale cullered & soe you may use it as you please.

3 To know when yr sugar is in A full Sirrup x

After yr sugar is in a thin sirrup set it to boyle againe, & in ye boyling it will change its culler and looke high cullered like strong beare, & then it is in a full sirrup. & soe you may use it.

of the utmost importance and usually constituted the sole adornment. Flowers seem seldom to have been used. Fine pieces of silver occasionally ornamented the table, and we know that Thomas Jefferson, the Washingtons, and John Adams each possessed a *plateau de dessert.* The Washingtons' is still preserved at Mount Vernon; the "images," however, belong to a descendant. Ornaments of this kind were, however, very rare.

It was more usual for five large platters, containing the *pièces de résistance,* to be placed crosswise the length of the table. A tureen of soup at each end, which began the dinner, was replaced by fish. At right angles to the chief dishes were set smaller platters and dishes with the sauces, vegetables, "made dishes," and food of secondary importance. Many of the old cook books contain engravings showing the proper arrangement of a table. Great elaboration and ingenuity were often employed, and elaborate designs of ovals and circles resulted. It was a point of etiquette that the tablecloth should scarcely be visible. Precise rules for setting the table were laid down by all the old authorities. "For two Dishes," says one, "the best shaped Table is a pretty long Square, such as will hold one at each End and two on each Side; and the Dishes are placed one near the Top, and the other near the Bottom, with Room for Plates between, as at the Sides, only less. For three Dishes, the Table should be a broader Square, but still oblong; and one Dish is placed at the Top, and two Side by Side at the Bottom; this is a very awkward Method: But three is an odd Number; two upon the Table at once, and one of them removed, does better. A Dinner of four Dishes is set upon the Table thus; there is one at the Top, one at the Bottom, and one on each Side, a vacant Space being left in the Middle; this also has a raw Appearance, and the Vacancy should be filled up with something."

The service likewise differed from what would today be considered fashionable. The food was put on the table by servants, who changed the china and silver as necessary; but the serving and carving were done by the host and hostess, even though four or five men servants were in attendance, as was the case at Washington's table. The servants had their function, however trivial. "It was our custom," says an Emily Post of 1790, "to let the Lady of the House help her Visitors; and this, though troublesome to her, was founded upon Reason. She was supposed to understand carving perfectly well, and to know where the best Bit lay; it also gave her an Opportunity of showing with what Satisfaction she waited on her Friends. At present the Fashion is, that every one takes Care of himself, helping himself to what is next, or sending his Plate to the Person who sits near what he likes; so that the Lady fares like the rest of the Company, and has no more trouble than others. This is Civility to her, because it excuses her a great deal of Trouble, but it takes from her the Opportunity of serving her Friends. The Company are meant to be entertained, and the better they are so, the more the Master of the House will be pleased. They were under a Constraint, when everything was to come from the Hand of the Mistress; they did not care to shew they had large Stomachs, or they were ashamed to speak, or they were sorry to give her Trouble; so that half of them did not dine well. Now every one helps himself as he likes, and where he likes; nobody sees what he eats, and if he gives anybody trouble, he is in the Way of returning it, by helping them in his Turn to any that is next him."

Under these circumstances, carving naturally became not only a fine art but actually a rite, and all the old cook books devote an elaborate chapter to laying bare its mysteries. Who of us moderns could pass a test on how to rear a goose, unbrace a mallard or duck, unlace a coney, wing a partridge, allay a pheasant, dismember a hen, thigh a woodcock, display a crane, or lift a swan? Our struggles with a leg of lamb or a roast of beef, when we are brave enough to attempt even that, seem trifling in the face of all this.

The dinner for which so much knowledge was a preliminary was indeed an imposing affair. Although nominally of only two courses, there were so many dishes in each course that we wonder how it was possible to taste even the half. One sometimes feels that in these dinners American cookery had proceeded on the principle enunciated by a famous gourmet, that it is very easy to entertain a numerous company with healthy appetites. To learn what was actually served, we once more turn to the old cook books, for many of them print model menus for the assistance of the perplexed housewife. A dinner suitable for the month of February, in the year 1792, would be composed in the following manner.

FIRST COURSE

Small Chicken Patties	Soup Puree removed with Salmon	Pork Cutlets Sauce Robert
Red Cabbage Stew'd		Lobster Sauce
Boil'd Chickens	Shoulder of Mutton in Epigram	Masht Potatoes
Plain Butter		Boil'd Turkey
Shrimp Sauce	Ham	French Beans Fricaseed
Drest Greens	Beef Tremblongue	
Scotch Collops		Celery Sauce
	Soup Santea removed with Stew'd Carp	Oyster Loaves

SECOND COURSE

Maids of Honor	2 Wild Ducks	Rhenish Cream
Asparagus à la Pettit Poi		Prawns
	Lambs Tails au Beshemel	Sauce
Sauce		Plovers
2 Teal	Hare Roasted	
		Sauce
Crayfish		
Sauce	Sweetbreads à la dauphin	Chardoons Fricaseed
Fruit in Jellie	3 Partridges	Custards

After the second course, the cloth was removed from the table, fresh glasses and decanters of wine were set on, along with fruit and nuts, the ladies retired, and the real business of the evening began. As a rule, dinner parties were confined almost exclusively to men; occasionally the wife of the host was present, and sometimes other women, but this was rather unusual.

With the coming of the nineteenth century, the number of courses at a dinner party seems to have increased to three; for in the American edition of her famous cook book, published in Alexandria, Virginia, in 1805, Mrs. Glasse, the Fanny Farmer of the eighteenth century, gives the order of a modern bill of fare for each month in the manner the dishes are to be placed upon the table. For January we find:

FIRST COURSE

Leg of Lamb	Soup	Boiled Chickens
Chicken and	Petit Patties	Roasted Beef
Veal Pie		
	Cod's Head	Scotch Collops
Tongue	Patties	
	Vermicelli Soup	

SECOND COURSE

	Roasted Turkey	
Marinated Smelts	Tartles	Mince Pies
Roast Sweetbreads	Stands of jellies	Larks
Almond Tort	Maids of Honour	Lobsters

THIRD COURSE

	Morels	
	Dutch Beef	
Artichoke Bottoms	Cut Pastry	Macaroni
Custards	Potted Chars.	Black Caps
Scalloped Oysters	Rabbit Fricaseed	Stewed Celery

The roasts, the fowle, the "pyes," the tarts, the preserves, the jellies, and the cakes-in short, the many delicacies that covered the ample table at Mount Vernon-were all prepared in the steep-roofed white kitchen building connected with the mansion by a colonnade. It was usual on Virginia plantations to have the kitchen in a separate building, and Mount Vernon was no exception. With fourteen house servants, this presented no difficulty, and the Washingtons were doubtless not obliged to resort to the "batter cake express" to carry the steaming food to the table.

The cooking was carried on under conditions that would seem to us to present insuperable difficulties. Stoves were, of course, unknown, and everything-stewing, boiling, broiling, and baking-was accomplished in the huge fireplace. In it were the hangers to which the pots and kettles were hung by the pot hooks and the roasting jack. Near at hand were the countless implements employed by the cook of the period: pot racks, spit racks, a Dutch oven, frying and dripping pans, a mortar and pestle, gridirons, trivets, special pans for sauces, stews, preserves, and pickles, a coffee roaster and mill, spice mortars, tart moulds, graters, skimmers, and ladles of various sizes.

Cumbersome and difficult as the cooking methods of Martha Washington's day may seem to us, they presented no difficulties to the housewife of the period, for she knew nothing else. She knew, however, many things that have been lost to us. She knew that fire was not just fire and heat not just heat. She knew what flavor would be imparted by the smoke of hickory, pine, sassafras, red or white oak, and even the humble corn cob. She knew which woods would produce a quick fire and which a lazy one. With her lore and her knowledge, she achieved a mellowness and richness of flavor which we can never acquire when we reach out a hand to press the button that releases our modern and ineffective giants, gas and electricity.

Martha Washington's cook book is presented, not as an historical curiosity, but as a usable cook book. It is not a comprehensive collection of recipes, treating of all the varied phases of cooking; it is, rather, a collection of the favorite dishes and "rules" of the Washington household. It has been necessary, of course, to make some adaptation of the recipes. The quantities had to be brought in line with what we consider a normal amount for serving six persons. Furthermore, some of the recipes are scarcely in accordance with modern taste or practice. To bake meat or fish in pools of blood, with careful directions for semidecapitating the creature and permitting him to come to a slow and sorry end, is a performance that would not ordinarily be undertaken in a modern kitchen. Neither did it seem necessary to preface the directions for cooking fish with the words, "take out ye guts, lungs and all that is within," something we have long learned to leave to the skill of the fishman.

Certain recipes were obviously written carelessly or in haste, with ingredients omitted or added as an afterthought at the end. By comparison with similar recipes in other cook books of this period, the missing ingredients could usually be detected and included.

Various terms and phrases, along with the archaic spelling, bring vividly to mind that two centuries have passed since Martha Washington's cook book was written. It is directed, for instance, that meat and fish should be garnished with sops and sippets, the ancient and more hearty equivalent of what we today designate as toast points. The sops were usually moistened with some of the liquid in which the meat or fish was cooked, and thus not only deserve their name but appear as the logical ancestor of the bread and gravy beloved by children (and not a few grown-ups) ever since.

Again, the writer of the Washington cook book is careful to specify that cakes and fritters should be fried in "good butter," a silent commentary on the lack of refrigeration as well as on the wild onion rampant in the spring. In sweets, suet is often used where we should employ butter, and this substitution may readily be made. In certain cakes, barm was the leavening agent. Barm is probably unknown to nine out of ten people, and impossible to buy. It is the foam that rises to the top of fermenting malt liquors. The present-day equivalent, in soda or baking-powder, has been substituted.

Although the housewife of today is more given to buying her jams and jellies at a chain store than to sweltering over a preserve kettle, a few of Martha Washington's rules for preserving have been -given. Canning, as we understand it, was an unknown art. jellies were made, but marmalade and quidoneys, or pastes, were the real favorites. Everything available on the farm was put to use; all the fruits and berries, including barberries, and almost every flower was pressed into service. Thus we find a "marmalet of mulberries," preserved rosebuds and gilliflowers, candied "marrygoulds," "apricock cakes," mint cakes, pickled "lettice stalks," pickled broom buds, and so on. A few of the more practical of these recipes have been given; the large majority, however, are omitted.

Every household in Martha Washington's time made its own wines, shrubs, syrups, and cordials. Here again we find all varieties of fruits and flowers used. The stouter beverages-such as mead, made by fermenting a mixture of honey and water, and metheglin, a spiced version of mead; to say nothing of Usequebath, a variety of Irish whisky-were not neglected. For those hardy souls who would like to be fully imbued with the spirit of bygone days, a few of these recipes are appended.

SOUPS

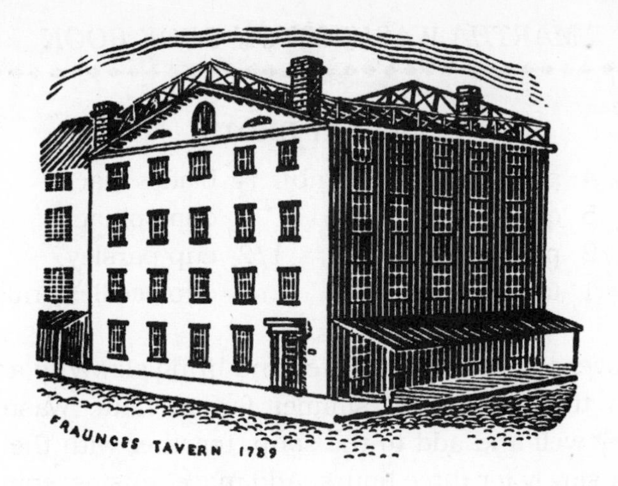

SOUPS

TO MAKE FRENCH BROTH

2	pounds beef	1	pound spinach
1	pound clear veal	1	small head of lettuce
1	hen	1/2	pound skirt steak
	Whole mace	2	tablespoons butter
1/2	small cabbage	1	tablespoon salt

1/4 teaspoon pepper-corns

Put in a soup kettle beef suitable for soups (short ribs, brisket, or shank), veal cut in cubes, and hen, disjointed. Cover with cold water and bring to a boil. Let boil five minutes; then remove scum. Add mace, cabbage cut in quarters, spinach, lettuce cut in quarters, salt, and peppercorns. Simmer for four or five hours. Meanwhile cut the skirt steak in small cubes and brown in butter. Add a little of the broth, cover, and simmer until tender. Strain the soup and serve with the cubes of beef in it.

BARLEY BROTH

- 4 pounds neck of lamb
- 5 quarts water
- 1/2 pound barley
- 1 tablespoon salt
- 4 blades mace
- 1 cup spinach
- 1/2 cup parsley
- 1 cup seedless raisins

Cover the meat with water and bring slowly to a boil. Skim thoroughly and simmer for an hour. Wash the barley well and add to the soup, together with the salt. Cook slowly for three hours. Add mace, raisins, spinach, and chopped parsley, and cook for another hour.

FRENCH POTTAGE

- 3 pounds short ribs of beef
- 1 marrow bone
- 2 pounds neck of veal or lamb
- 1 pound spinach
- 1 small cabbage
- 2 pounds fresh peas
- Salt
- 1 teaspoon pepper-corns
- Toast strips
- Yolks of 3 eggs

Put the beef in a soup kettle and cover with cold water. Bring to a boil and remove scum. Cook slowly for an hour. Add neck of veal or lamb cut in pieces and the marrow bone, and simmer for two or three hours. An hour before serving add the spinach leaves, the cabbage cut in eighths, salt, pepper-corns, and the peas.

Butter five slices of bread cut in strips and brown in the oven. Cover the bottom of serving dish with bread and pour two cupfuls of the broth over it. When well soaked, fill the dish with the vegetables and bits of meat and some broth. Beat the yolks of three eggs and add gradually two cups of broth. Pour on the former and serve.

FRENCH POTTAGE, ANOTHER WAY

2 ducks	1/2 cup gravy
1 cup strong stock	1/4 cup white wine
4 carrots	4 anchovies
1 small cabbage	Salt
Whole mace	Pepper

Fried parsley

Clean and dress two ducks. Put in roasting pan, dust with salt and pepper, and bake in hot oven for forty-five minutes. Then add stock, mace, carrots cut in neat squares, and cabbage cut in quarters. Cover pan and set on top of stove to finish cooking. When the ducks and cabbage are tender, in about half an hour, remove ducks to hot platter and dice cabbage. Return to liquid in pan, add gravy (any kind that is on hand), white wine, and anchovies cut in small pieces. Let cook up. Then pour the broth with cabbage and carrots over the ducks and decorate the dish with sprigs of fried parsley.

PORRIDGE OF GREEN PEAS

2 cups young green peas	1 teaspoon sugar
Sprig of mint	1 tablespoon flour
1 teaspoon salt	2 cups milk
2 cups boiling water	2 tablespoons butter

Black pepper

Drop peas into boiling water. Add sugar, salt, and mint. Cook slowly until peas are tender. Rub through a sieve. Add milk and bring to boil. Mix the flour and butter, and thicken soup with this. Add more salt, if necessary, and freshly ground black pepper to taste.

PLUM, OR STEWED BROTH

- 3 pounds short ribs of beef
- 2 pounds marrow bone
- 3 quarts water
- 1 tablespoon salt
- 1 teaspoon sugar
- 3 blades mace
- 2/3 cup currants
- 1/2 pound prunes
- 3/4 cup bread crumbs
- 2/3 cup seedless raisins

Cut the meat in pieces and put in a saucepan with the salt and cold water. Bring slowly to a boil, skim thoroughly, and let simmer for three hours. Soak the prunes and currants. Remove pits from former and add to broth with the bread and sugar. Simmer two hours more. Remove the meat and serve. A little yellow coloring may be added.

WHITE BROTH

- 1 capon
- 1 blade of mace
- 2 quarts water
- 1 small onion
- 2 carrots
- 1/2 bay leaf
- 2 tablespoons raisins
- 2 tablespoons currants
- Sprig of parsley
- Sprig of thyme
- 1/2 teaspoon pepper-corns
- 1 cup cream
- Yolks of 4 eggs

Wash and disjoint the capon. Put in a pan with the salt and water, bring to a boil, skim, and simmer for three hours. Add the other seasonings and cook one hour more. Remove the meat, strain soup, and let cool. Remove any fat. Add the cream and, at the last moment, the well-beaten egg yolks. Serve at once.

WHITE BROTH, ANOTHER WAY

1 quart veal or mutton broth
1/8 teaspoon each cinnamon and nutmeg
Blade of mace
Salt to taste
1 cup prunes
1 cup currants
2/3 cup white wine
Yolks of 3 eggs
Small squares of toast

Take the broth in which a leg of mutton or veal has been cooked; there should be one quart. Soak the prunes and currants; cook separately and slowly until tender. Remove the stones from the prunes and cut lengthwise in strips. Add the wine and fruit to the soup. When it comes to a boil, pour it very carefully on the yolks of the eggs, which have been well beaten. Serve at once with small squares of buttered toast. Capon broth may be made the same way and the soup served with the capon cut in small pieces.

A GRUEL OF FRENCH BARLEY

1 tablespoon barley
1 quart cream
Blade of mace
4 tablespoons sugar
1/8 teaspoon salt
2 eggs
Rose water (optional)

Wash the barley and cook in water an hour or more, until tender. Add the cream, sugar, salt, and mace. Bring to the boiling point and pour over two well-beaten eggs. Add the rose water, if desired, and serve.

PEAS PORRIDGE OF DRIED PEAS

1 cup dried split peas
3 quarts cold water
1 tablespoon coriander seed
1/2 teaspoon ground pepper
1/2 teaspoon sugar
1 1/2 teaspoons salt
2 small onions
4 sprigs of parsley
1 tablespoon dried spearmint
1/4 pound butter

Pick over the peas, wash well, cover with cold water, and soak three hours. Drain and put in a saucepan. Add water, salt, sugar, pepper, coriander seed, which has been crushed or ground, parsley, spearmint, and onions, cut up fine. Simmer three or four hours. Pass through a sieve. Add the butter, let it boil up, and serve with croutons. "If you love it," this recipe concludes, "put in a little elder vinegar."

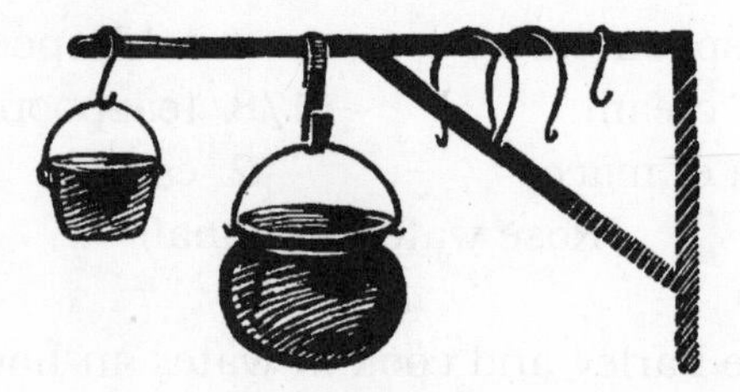

FISH

FISH

General Washington was very fond of fish, and a great deal of it appeared upon the table at Mount Vernon. We know that he was partial to shad, yet no recipe for shad appears in the *Cook Book.* The colored cooks were doubtless familiar with it and needed no special directions. On the other hand, we find various recipes for trout, haddock, and carp, the last a fish esteemed as a food in Europe but rare in America today. Recipes are likewise to be found for tench, a fish similar to carp; for roaches, another European fresh-water fish of the carp variety, on the order of spots; for eels and lampreys, an eel-like fish; and for whiting, a name used in various localities for different kinds of fish, such as sunfish or butter-fish. The sole referred to in the *Cook Book* is, of course, the sole found in European waters but not available in this country. Filet of flounder, the usual sole of America, can readily be substituted. Similarly, bluefish, mackerel, or other ordinary fish can be cooked according to the recipes given for the more exotic varieties.

The Washington household enjoyed shrimps and oysters, but no mention is made of terrapin, crabs, either hard or soft, clams, or any other shellfish.

BOILED SPOTS

6	spots		Sprig of thyme
1	tablespoon vinegar		Sprig of parsley
2	blades of mace	1/2	cup butter
1	teaspoon salt		Few pepper-corns

Toast points

Take the fattest spots you can get. Wash well and drop into boiling water to cover well. Add salt, vinegar, pepper, and herbs, and boil until the fish is tender, turning once. Drain well, remove to a hot platter and sprinkle with chopped parsley. Have the butter well creamed. Add one-half cup of the fish liquor and pour around as a sauce. Garnish with toast points.

FRIED SOLE

6	individual fillets of sole	5	tablespoons butter
6	anchovies, not rolled	1/4	cup white wine
	Salt and pepper	1	tablespoon lemon juice
	Parsley	1/2	teaspoon vinegar

Wash and dry the fillets. Dust with salt and freshly ground black pepper. Melt three tablespoons of butter in a frying pan; gently lay in the fillets and fry until a delicate brown, first on one side, then on the other. Sprinkle lemon.juice over them. Remove to a hot platter garnished with parsley and sliced lemon. Lay an anchovy lengthwise along in the center of each fillet. Brown two tablespoons butter; add wine, vinegar, salt to taste, and chopped parsley, and use as sauce.

ROAST FISH

- 1 shad, bluefish or mackerel
- 1 cup bread crumbs
- 1 cup melted butter
- 2 tablespoons water
- 1/2 teaspoon thyme
- Salt and pepper
- 1 tablespoon lemon juice
- 1 tablespoon capers

Wash the fish well, dry, and dust with salt and pepper. Season bread crumbs with salt, pepper, thyme, and one-half cup melted butter and water. Stuff the fish with this and sew up. Place in a buttered baking pan and bake for forty-five minutes in a hot oven, basting often with a little melted butter mixed with hot water. Remove to a hot platter. Mix the lemon juice and capers with remaining half cup of melted butter, let froth up, and pour over the fish. Any fish suitable for baking may be cooked this way. The original recipe calls for carp.

STEWED OYSTERS

1 pint oysters	3 pepper-corns
1 small white onion	Blade of mace
Salt	1/2 cup white wine

2 tablespoons butter

Clean oysters and reserve liquor. Drop oysters into a pan of boiling water, bring to a boil, turn immediately into a colander, and pour cold water on them. This will plump them and prevent them from shrinking. Mix the oyster liquor with the wine; add onion, salt, pepper, and mace. Add the oysters and cook a few minutes until edges curl. Add butter and serve.

STEWED HADDOCK

3 pounds of haddock	1 teaspoon salt
2 nutmegs	Pepper-corns
3 small white onions	Sprig of parsley

Wash the fish carefully, sprinkle with salt and drop in a pan containing one and a half quarts boiling water, salt, two nutmegs, cut in quarters, parsley, onions and a few pepper-corns. Boil gently until tender, about thirty minutes, turning once while cooking. Remove to a hot platter garnished with thin slices of lemon dotted with capers, and pour Sauce for Haddock over the fish.

BOILED TROUT

1	trout	1/8	teaspoon ginger
1 1/2	cups white wine		Sprig of rosemary
	Salt and pepper	2	tablespoons butter

Toast points

Wash the trout well and dry, rub with salt and pepper. Bring the wine to a boil, add spices and butter, and drop in the fish. Cook slowly until tender, about half an hour. Turn once during cooking. Remove to a hot platter, garnish with toast points and chopped parsley. Serve with maître d'hôtel butter–a modern touch.

BUTTERED SHRIMPS

1	pound green shrimp	Freshly ground black pepper
3/4	cup butter	
	Salt	Piece of bay leaf

1 carrot

Wash the shrimp. Drop in a pan of boiling salted water, to which has been added the bay leaf and carrot, cut in quarters. Cook for twenty minutes. Remove from fire and drain. Peel and remove the intestinal vein. Place shrimp in top of a double boiler to heat thoroughly. Cream the butter until light and fluffy. Turn shrimp onto a hot platter, cover with the butter, and strew with freshly ground black pepper.

STEWED CARP

1 carp	Sprig of rosemary
Salt	Sprig of parsley
Pepper-corns	1/2 nutmeg
2 tablespoons butter	1/2 cup vinegar

Wash the fish thoroughly. Drop into boiling water nearly to cover, to which has been added the salt, pepper, rosemary, parsley, nutmeg and butter. Cook until tender, turning several times. Drain well and place on a hot platter. Sprinkle with chopped parsley and surround with triangles of buttered toast which have been slightly moistened with the broth from the fish. Serve with Sauce for Carp. A pike or any other fish suitable for boiling may be cooked this way.

FISH PIE

1 pound preferred fish	3/4 cup artichoke bottoms
1 pint oysters	
2 tablespoons capers	1/2 pound mushrooms
Sprig of thyme	4 hard-boiled eggs
3 sprigs of parsley	1 1/2 cups mutton gravy
1/4 pound butter	
1 tablespoon vinegar	Salt and pepper

Pastry

Fillet of sole makes a delicious pie. It should be poached in court bouillon for eight minutes and then cut in strips. Add to it the oysters, which have been set on the fire to simmer until the edges curl, the capers, thyme, parsley, artichoke bottoms, eggs cut in eighths, mushrooms which have been sliced and cooked gently for ten minutes, salt and pepper. Add the vinegar to the gravy and moisten the fish mixture with it. Line a deep dish with pastry and dot with half the butter. Fill with the mixture and add remaining butter. Cover with a top crust of puff paste and bake until a golden brown.

STEWED TROUT

1 large trout
White wine
2 sprigs of thyme
2 sprigs of parsley
1 sprig of sweet marjoram
6 anchovies
1 teaspoon salt
Few pepper-corns
1/2 pound butter
Toast points

Have the fish cleaned, scaled, and well washed. Put in a saucepan together with the salt, pepper, herbs, and enough white wine to cover. Bring quickly to a boil; reduce heat and simmer until tender, turning once. Cream the butter, add anchovies cut in small bits, and beat well. Remove the fish to a hot platter. Mix the butter and anchovies with a cup of wine in which the fish has stewed. Pour over the fish and surround with toast points.

STEWED EELS

2	eels	1	blade mace
	Water	1/2	cup currants
	Vinegar		Bunch of sweet herbs
1/2	teaspoon salt	2	tablespoons butter
1/4	teaspoon nutmeg		Yolks of 2 eggs

Cut the eels in pieces about three or four inches long. Place in a pan and cover with a mixture of half vinegar and half water. Add salt, spices, currants, and sweet herbs, and stew slowly until tender. Remove to a hot platter. Add butter to the gravy and, lastly, stir in the well-beaten egg yolks. Pour over the eels and serve.

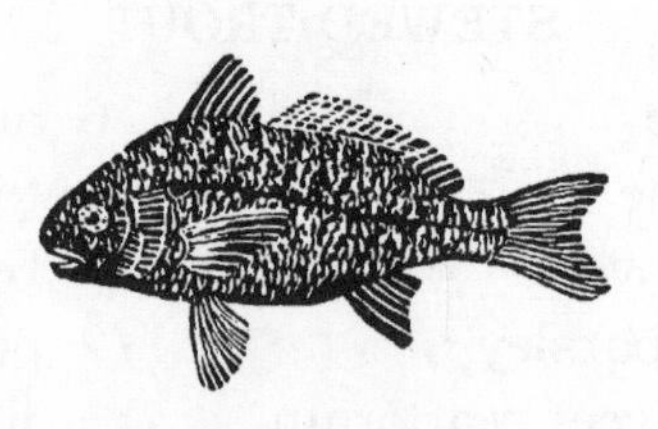

MEATS

THE BANQUET HALL, MOUNT VERNON

MEATS

Mutton seems to have been the favored meat at Mount Vernon. There are a dozen recipes for mutton, with veal a close second. Beef was more rarely used. The same holds true of the Old Dominion today. Capon and "chickin" were prime favorites, and pigeons, sparrow, venison, and hare also appear. True to the English tradition, boiling and stewing were the preferred methods of cooking meat, perhaps because the accomplishment was simpler. "To stew beefe stakes" may sound unorthodox to American ears, but the result is not as unfortunate as one might think. The roasting was, of course, done on spits before the open fire.

Stews and hash were familiar, as well as collops. Collops was a favorite dish from the fifteenth to the nineteenth centuries, although at the present time it is outmoded, at least in name. It usually meant a dish of meat cut in small pieces and warmed in gravy-in other words, a stew.

TO BAKE RUMP OF BEEF

- 4 pounds rump of beef
- 1 cup bread crumbs
- 4 hard-boiled eggs
- Thyme
- Winter savory
- Marjoram
- 2 tablespoons chopped parsley
- Salt and pepper
- 1/2 cup melted butter
- 2 white onions
- 1 cup boiling water
- Toast points

Have the butcher cut the beef so that there will be a pocket for stuffing. Chop the eggs fine and mix with bread crumbs. Add salt, pepper, thyme, savory, and marjoram to taste-about one half teaspoon of each-and one and a half tablespoons parsley. Stir in the melted butter. Stuff the beef with this and sew up. Place in roasting pan with the onions, cut up fine, one teaspoon of chopped parsley and one half teaspoon savory. Place in hot oven. When brown, add boiling water, reduce heat, and bake until tender, basting every fifteen minutes with liquor in pan. Remove to hot platter. Thicken gravy, if desired, with a little flour. Pour over meat and surround with toast points.

TO MAKE RED DEER OF BEEF

- 3 pounds top of round of beef
- 1/2 teaspoon nutmeg
- 1/4 teaspoon ginger
- 1 teaspoon salt
- 1/2 teaspoon peppercorns
- 1 pint claret
- 1/2 cup vinegar
- 1/2 cup water
- 1 bay leaf
- 2 tablespoons butter
- 1/2 teaspoon sugar
- Flour

Have the butcher lard the beef well. Rub it over with salt, ginger, and nutmeg. Place in a bowl and cover with the claret and vinegar. Add bay leaf, pepper-corns, and water. Let stand two days, turning twice a day. When ready to cook, dry off the meat. Melt butter in a Dutch oven and brown meat quickly. Reduce heat and add two cups of liquor in which meat has soaked. Cover and cook very slowly until tender, turning frequently. Add sugar to gravy and thicken with a little flour dissolved in water. "A neat's tongue soe seasoned is excellent good meat, & all soe Veale," our recipe concludes.

ANOTHER WAY TO MAKE BEEF LIKE RED DEER

3 pounds round of beef
Nutmeg
Pepper and salt
3 bay leaves
1/2 pint white wine
1/2 pint vinegar
1 cup butter
Pastry

Have the butcher lard the beef and pound it well with the flat of his knife. Season it with salt, pepper, and grated nutmeg. Place in a bowl and cover it with the white wine and vinegar. Let stand twenty-four hours, turning several times. Prepare a rich pastry and line a round baking dish with it. Break up the bay leaves and put half on the pastry. Remove meat from wine and put in the pastry shell. Put remaining bay leaves on top. Dot over with one half cup butter. Cover with top crust; make a few incisions with a knife and bake in a moderate oven for four hours. On removing from oven, lift up top crust, or make incision, and add remaining one half cup butter.

BOILED RUMP OF BEEF

3 pounds rump of beef
Boiling water
Large bunch of pot-herbs
1 tablespoon salt
1/2 teaspoon pepper-corns
4 white onions
6 carrots
White wine
Toast points

Wipe off the meat and put in kettle. Pour on enough boiling water nearly to cover it. Add the potherbs, pepper-corns, salt, and the onions, cut fine. Boil gently for one and a half hours. Cut the carrots in quarters and add. Continue boiling for four or five hours. Remove to hot platter. Season a good cupful of the broth with white wine to taste and pour around the meat. Garnish with toast points.

STEWED BEEF STEAKS

2 1/2 pounds fillet of beef
Sprig of thyme
Sprig of mint
Savory
3 sprigs of parsley
Salt and pepper
2 anchovies
3 white onions
1 tablespoon vinegar
1 cup boiling water
Rounds of toast

Have the beef larded and cut in slices one half inch thick. Put in a pan and add water, vinegar, salt and pepper, the herbs and spices, and the anchovies and onions, chopped very fine. Bring quickly to a boil; then simmer until tender, turning often. Serve on rounds of toast and pour the gravy over them.

BAKED SHOULDER OF LAMB

3 1/2 pounds shoulder of lamb
2 teaspoons dried thyme
Salt and pepper
3 tablespoons butter
1 cup claret
2 tablespoons flour

Have the butcher bone the lamb. Rub it over with salt and pepper and thyme. Form into a roll and tie. Rub the outside of meat with flour, and salt, and pepper. Melt the butter in a Dutch oven and brown the meat. Reduce heat and add claret and a pinch of thyme. Cook slowly until tender. Thicken the gravy with a little flour if necessary.

SHOULDER OF MUTTON ROASTED WITH GARLIC

3 1/2 pounds shoulder of mutton or lamb
2 cloves of garlic
Salt and pepper
1 cup claret
Few gratings nutmeg
Flour

Bone and roll a shoulder of mutton or lamb. Pour boiling water over garlic and insert in the lamb. Place meat in roasting pan, dust with salt and pepper, and put in a hot oven to brown. Add claret and a few gratings of nutmeg, and baste with this. A little water may be added if necessary. Remove meat to hot platter. Thicken the gravy with a little flour dissolved in water and pour around meat.

A GRAND LEG OF LAMB

1	large leg of lamb	1/2	cup melted butter
1	cup bread crumbs		Salt
1/2	teaspoon thyme		Pepper
1/4	teaspoon marjoram	1/2	cup white wine
1/4	teaspoon grated nutmeg	1	pair of sweetbreads
1/4	teaspoon chopped lemon rind	1	pair of lamb kidneys
		12	sausages
1	tablespoon capers		Yolks 2 eggs
6	anchovies	1	tablespoon flour
4	hard-boiled eggs		Toast points

Have the butcher remove bone from leg. Mix the bread crumbs with thyme, marjoram, nutmeg, pepper, salt, lemon rind, capers, and four anchovies, cut up. Add melted butter. Stuff the lamb with this mixture and secure it with skewers or sew it up. Rub the meat with salt and a little grated nutmeg. Surround with white wine. Put in hot oven and baste with the wine every twenty minutes. When brown, reduce the heat somewhat.

Meanwhile, parboil the sweetbreads, cut them in strips, and brown lightly in butter. Trim the kidneys, split, and broil ten minutes. Arrange the sausages on the same broiler and broil while kidneys are cooking, turning once. Remove lamb to platter and arrange sweetbreads, kidneys, and sausages about it. Garnish the platter with toast points and little mounds of finely chopped hardboiled egg.

Cut two anchovies in fine pieces and add to the gravy. Dissolve flour in a small amount of water and thicken the gravy with this. Add the beaten egg yolks at the last moment.

TO STEW A NECK OF MUTTON WITH ORANGES

- 3 pounds neck of lamb or mutton
- Salt and pepper
- Grated nutmeg
- 1/2 tablespoon vinegar
- Juice Of 5 oranges
- 2 oranges, grated rinds
- Flour
- 3 tablespoons butter
- 1/2 cup seedless raisins

Have the meat cut in pieces suitable for stewing. Roll in flour, seasoned with salt and pepper and grated nutmeg. Melt butter in a Dutch oven and brown the meat in this. Mix the vinegar with orange juice and grated rind of 2 oranges. Cover and let simmer until tender. When nearly done, add the raisins.

TO BOIL A BREAST OF MUTTON

- 3 pounds breast of lamb or mutton
- 1/4 teaspoon thyme
- 1/4 teaspoon marjoram
- Salt and pepper
- 1 tablespoon capers
- 1 tablespoon chopped parsley
- 1/4 teaspoon grated nutmeg
- 1 tablespoon butter

Have the butcher cut the meat in small pieces. Put in pan and add salt, pepper, capers, herbs, and spices. Nearly cover the meat with boiling water. Bring quickly to a boil and let boil five minutes; then skim. Reduce heat and let simmer until the meat is tender. A tablespoon of butter may be added. The meat may be eaten with the broth or removed to a platter and served with caper or tomato sauce, a modern improvement.

TO BOIL A NECK OF MUTTON

3 pounds neck of lamb or mutton	2 tablespoons butter
Small bunch of parsley	1/2 tablespoon vinegar
1 whole mace	1/2 teaspoon sugar
Pepper-corns	1 teaspoon salt
	Flour

Have the butcher cut the neck of lamb in small pieces, as for stew. Put it in a pan, nearly cover with boiling water, and add mace, salt, pepper-corns, and parsley. Let simmer until tender. Remove to platter and serve covered with the Sauce for Boiled Mutton.

TO STEW A LEG OF MUTTON OR ROAST IT

1 leg mutton or lamb	1/2 tablespoon vinegar
6 hard-boiled eggs	2/3 cup water
1/2 teaspoon thyme	1 teaspoon sugar
1/4 teaspoon rosemary	Salt and pepper
1/2 cup dried currants	Flour

Have the butcher remove the hip bone of a leg of lamb, thus forming a pocket. Chop the hard-boiled eggs and add salt, pepper, thyme, and rosemary. Stuff the lamb with this and close with skewers or sew it up. Rub meat with salt and pepper, and place in a roasting pan. Put in a hot oven. Baste with fat in pan every twenty minutes. When brown add water and continue basting until done. It will take about an hour and three-quarters. Remove meat to platter. To the gravy add vinegar and currants, which have been soaked in warm water to make them plump. If the gravy has cooked away much, a little water may be added. Thicken gravy with about two teaspoons flour dissolved in a very little water.

This meat may be boiled instead of roasted. In that case place in a kettle, cover with boiling water, and bring quickly to a boil. Let it cook hard for three minutes, then remove the scum. Reduce heat and let simmer until tender. When half done, add one tablespoon salt and a few pepper-corns. When done, remove the meat to a platter and serve with caper sauce. The broth may have three tablespoons of rice cooked in it and be used as soup.

TO STEW A NECK OR LOIN OF MUTTON

- 3 pounds neck of lamb
  or
- 2 pounds loin of lamb
- 1 teaspoon salt
- Black pepper
- Grated nutmeg
- Grated mace
- 1 scant tablespoon flour
- 1 tablespoon butter
- Vinegar
- 1 tablespoon chopped lemon peel
- 6 anchovies
- Toast points

Have the butcher cut a neck of mutton into small pieces suitable for stewing. It will weigh about three pounds. A two-pound loin of lamb may be used, cut into chops, but it is more expensive. Season the meat with salt, pepper, and grated nutmeg, which must be well rubbed in. Place meat in a saucepan or Dutch oven. Add sufficient water barely to cover, and let it stew slowly until tender and most of the water has evaporated. Season with vinegar to taste, about 1 tablespoon; add lemon peel cut in small pieces, anchovies, and grated mace. Mix butter and flour together and stir into the gravy to thicken. Serve on a platter surrounded with buttered toast points.

BROTH COLLOPS

Small leg of lamb	1/2	cup water
Butter		Juice of 1 lemon
Salt and pepper	3/4	cup white wine
	6	anchovies

Have the butcher cut a small leg of lamb in thin slices and pound it with the side of his knife. Put some butter in an iron skillet and brown the meat on both sides, adding more butter as needed. Place all the meat in a casserole, season with salt and pepper, add water, white wine, lemon juice, and anchovies, cut in small pieces. Cook slowly until tender. Serve with the broth.

SCOTCH COLLOPS

1	leg of lamb		Sweet marjoram
	or		Winter savory
3	pounds veal	1	onion
	or	1/2	cup dry bread cubes
3	pounds beef	1	tablespoon capers
	Vinegar	1	dozen oysters
1	pint strong stock	6	anchovies
1/2	pint water	2	tablespoons butter
	Salt and pepper		Triangles of bread
1	sprig of thyme		Sliced lemon

The collops may be made from lamb, veal or beef. If lamb, use a leg; if veal, a piece of the top of the leg, weighing four pounds; if beef, three pounds, top of the round.

Have the butcher cut the meat in thin slices and pound it with the flat of his knife. Marinate the meat in vinegar for several hours. Wipe it off, put it in an iron frying pan. Cover with stock and water. Season with salt, pepper, thyme, sweet marjoram, winter savory, and an onion. Let simmer until the meat is tender. Strain the gravy into a pan, add dry bread cut in small cubes, anchovies, capers, oysters, lemon juice, and butter. Let simmer until the consistency of gravy.

Place your meat on a platter, pour over it the sauce, surround with triangles of bread that have been browned in butter, and decorate with slices of lemon dotted with capers.

A STEWED DISH

- 2 pounds loin of veal or lamb
- 3/4 cup white wine
- Salt
- 1 tablespoon capers
- Yolks of 5 eggs
- 1 tablespoon chopped lemon rind
- 1/4 pound butter
- Sliced lemon
- Chopped parsley
- Toast points

Have the meat cut in slices nearly an inch thick. Remove fat, dust with salt, and pour white wine over it. Add capers and lemon rind. Nearly cover meat with boiling water. Let it come to a boil; then reduce heat and simmer until tender. Remove meat to hot platter. Add butter to gravy and let it melt. Stir into the gravy the egg yolks well beaten, taking care that they do not curdle. Pour over meat. Garnish with parsley and toast points.

A HASH OF MUTTON

1/2	leg cooked mutton or lamb	1	tablespoon vinegar
3	tablespoons capers	1	tablespoon flour
	Salt	1	tablespoon butter
1	cup water	6	anchovies

3 tablespoons lamb gravy

Cut the meat in tiny cubes, putting in some of the fat. Crack the bone and put in pan with the meat. Add the capers and water, and salt to taste. Stew slowly for twenty-five minutes. Remove bone. Cut the anchovies fine and add. Add vinegar and lamb gravy. Thicken with the butter and flour mixed together.

A HASH OF MUTTON OR VEAL

2	cups cold mutton or veal		Sprig of mint, fresh or dry
3	small white onions	3/4	tablespoon vinegar
2	tablespoons butter	1/2	cup chopped spinach
1	tablespoon capers		Salt

1 cup gravy

Cut either cold lamb or cold veal in very thin slices. Cut the onions fine and brown in the butter. Add the meat, capers, gravy, spinach, and mint. Pour the gravy over this, and add vinegar and salt, if needed. Simmer slowly for half an hour. A little water may be added if necessary.

A HASH OF VEAL

2	cups cold roast veal	1	cup claret
1	white onion	1	tablespoon butter
1	tablespoon capers	1	tablespoon flour
1/2	cup veal gravy		Toast points

Parsley

Cut the onion fine and brown in butter. Add the meat cut in tiny cubes, claret, capers, and veal gravy. Let simmer for twenty minutes. Mix butter with flour, and thicken the sauce with this. Add salt if necessary. Serve on a platter surrounded with toast points that have been dipped in melted butter and sprinkled with chopped parsley.

ROAST PIG

1	small pig		Bread crumbs
	Salt and pepper	3/4	cup butter
	Sprigs of thyme	1/2	teaspoon sugar

Thoroughly clean a young suckling pig. Dust over with salt. Put in hot oven. After about an hour, when half roasted, pull off the skin and stick the pig full of sprigs of thyme. Return to oven and baste frequently with three quarters cup butter, melted and mixed with a few coarse bread crumbs. It requires about two hours to roast the pig. Serve with Bread Sauce.

STUFFED LEG OF VEAL

5 pounds leg of veal
1 cup bread crumbs
Herbs
Yolks of 2 eggs
Lemon peel
Capers
Bacon for larding
1 tablespoon white wine vinegar
1/2 cup water
1 tablespoon butter
1 tablespoon flour
1/2 tablespoon chopped parsley
1 cup oysters
Salt and pepper
Mace
Grated nutmeg
4 hard-boiled eggs

Have the butcher bone the meat and prepare it for stuffing. If you are not experienced in larding, have him lard the fat side with thin strips of bacon. Prepare the stuffing by mixing the bread crumbs with a scant teaspoonful of whatever herbs you choose-thyme, summer savory, or marjoram-one half teaspoonful of salt, a dash of freshly ground black pepper, a little mace, and a little grated nutmeg. Add one tablespoon of capers and one half tablespoon of lemon peel chopped very fine. Cut up the soft part of the oysters and add. Beat the egg yolks well and mingle with the crumb mixture.

Stuff the meat with this and sew up. Sprinkle with salt and pepper, and put four slices of bacon over the top. Place in hot oven and roast until tender; it will take about three hours. Baste frequently with fat in pan. Remove bacon strips when they are brown, and add water. The pan may be covered after the meat has browned. Continue basting. When done, remove to a hot platter. To the gravy in the pan add white wine vinegar, one teaspoon finely chopped lemon peel, grated nutmeg, and flour mixed with butter. If the gravy is not the right consistency, a little water may be added.

Garnish the platter with chopped hard-boiled eggs, to which a little salt and pepper have been added.

TO SOUSE VEAL

4	pounds leg of veal	3	mace
1 1/2	quarts boiling water		Large sprig of parsley
2	teaspoons salt	2	white onions
	Pepper-corns	1	pint white wine
	Stalk celery	1/2	pint vinegar

Put meat in kettle, add water and salt, and boil until half done. Add wine, vinegar, herbs, and spices, and simmer until tender. Let meat stand in broth for three or four days in a cold place. Then remove and cut in thin slices. Serve cold.

OXFORD KATE'S SAUSAGES

3	pounds fresh ham or veal	1/2	tablespoon pepper
		1/2	tablespoon cloves
1	pound suet	1/2	tablespoon mace
1	tablespoon salt	1	tablespoon sage
		3	eggs

Grind meat and suet very fine and mix together. Add seasoning and eggs, omitting one egg white. Work all well together with the hands. Form into small rolls about the size of a finger. Fry in butter until a golden brown. "Theyr sauce is mustard," the manuscript directs.

TO STEW A BREAST OF VEAL

3	pounds breast of veal	1/2	cup cream
	Nutmeg	1	cup hot water
	Bunch of sweet herbs[1]	1/2	cup white wine
	Salt		Yolks 3 eggs
1	white onion		Sliced lemon

1 1/2 dozen large oysters

Have the meat cut in small pieces. Rub the meat with salt. Slice onion fine and put both in a stew pan, together with hot water and white wine. Add sweet herbs. Cover and let cook slowly until tender, about one hour. Remove meat to platter and keep warm. Add cream to gravy and then yolks of eggs. Do not boil. Strain gravy over meat, sprinkle with chopped parsley, and garnish with thin slices of lemon and oysters, which have been salted and cooked until the edges curl.

TO MAKE A FRICASSEE

1	stewing chicken, or	1	white onion
1	rabbit	2	tablespoons chopped parsley
	Flour		
1	teaspoon salt	1/2	teaspoon thyme
1/2	teaspoon pepper	1	cup water
3/4	cup butter		Yolks of 3 eggs

Juice of 1 lemon

The fricassee may be made with chicken or with rabbit. Disjoint the chicken or rabbit. Dust with flour, salt, and pepper, rubbing this well into the skin. Put

[1]Sweet herbs may include any of a dozen or more varieties, such as angelica, basil, caraway, fennel, hyssop, sweet marjoram, rosemary, summer savory, winter savory, sage, thyme, and even spinach. The choice is left to the cook.

butter into an iron frying pan or Dutch oven and let it melt. Add onion cut fine, parsley, and thyme. Then put in the chicken or rabbit and fry until a pale brown. Add a cupful of water, cover and let cook slowly until tender. Remove meat to platter. Beat the egg yolks together with the lemon juice. Stir mixture into the gravy very slowly so that it does not curdle. The gravy must be just below the boiling point. Strain gravy over meat and sprinkle with chopped parsley. Serve at once.

TO MAKE A FRICASSEE OF CHICKEN, LAMB, VEAL, OR RABBIT

1	stewing chicken	1/4	teaspoon mace
	or	1/4	teaspoon black pepper
3	pounds breast of lamb, or	1	teaspoon salt
2	pounds clear veal	1/2	cup butter
	or	1/2	cup white wine
1	rabbit	1/2	cup chicken stock
1/4	teaspoon cloves	1/2	teaspoon tarragon
1/4	teaspoon nutmeg		Yolks of 3 eggs
		1/2	cup cream

1 tablespoon chopped lemon peel

Disjoint chicken or rabbit, or bone lamb or veal. Mix together cloves, nutmeg, mace, salt, and pepper, and rub meat well with this. Melt the butter in a Dutch oven and brown the meat nicely. Add the stock and white wine, and let simmer until tender. Remove meat to a platter. Beat the egg yolks well. Add cream to gravy, and when it starts to bubble, stir in the eggs. Do not boil. Pour over meat and sprinkle with tarragon and chopped lemon peel.

STEWED CALVES' FEET

4 to 6 calves' feet	1/2 teaspoon cinnamon
1 tablespoon vinegar	1/4 teaspoon mace
1 teaspoon sugar	3/4 cup water
3 tablespoons currants	Butter

Wipe the calves' feet, put in boiling salted water, and boil one-half hour. Remove and skin them. Place in a pan with water, vinegar, sugar, spices, and currants, and simmer until tender. Add a good-sized piece of butter, about two tablespoons, and serve.

MEAT PIES

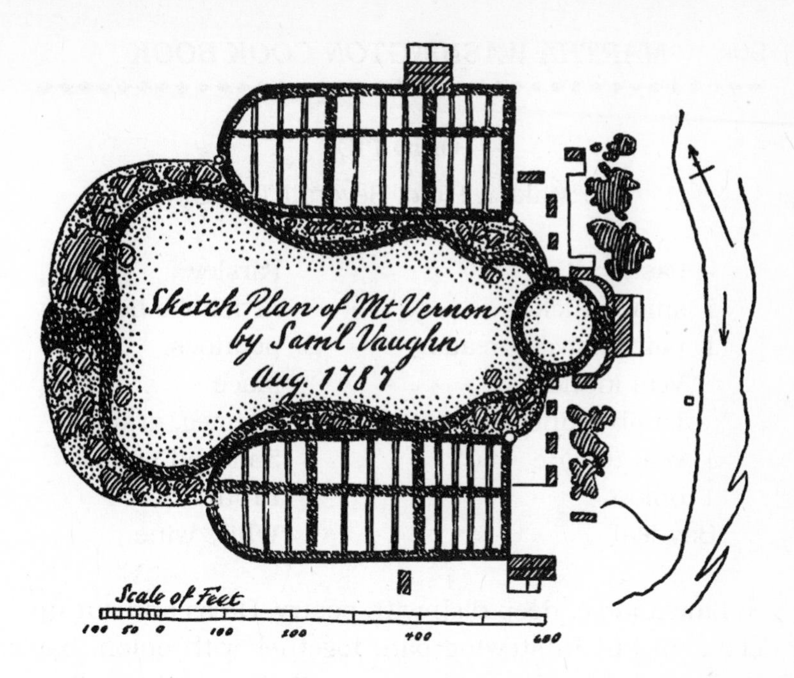

MEAT PIES

Meat pies were a much-loved dainty. The crust in which they were baked was known as "the coffin" and was usually made of puff paste. The filling might be of chicken, veal, bacon, pigeon, pork, sheep's tongue, or "of severall things." The cook might use her imagination and include spices, artichoke bottoms, hard-boiled eggs, and even sugar, rose water, and "raisins of ye sun." Others were more orthodox and made their meat pies with the usual meat, gravy, and spices.

OLIO PIE

(To Make a Pie of Severall Things)

	Pastry		Parsley
1	small chicken		Artichoke bottoms
1	pair of sweetbreads	2	potatoes
	Veal kidneys		Mace
	Lamb kidneys	1/2	nutmeg, grated
1	veal tongue		Salt and pepper
1	onion		Broth
	Bay leaf		White wine

Line a large, deep dish with pastry. Dress and cut up chicken. Put in stewing pan, together with onion, bay leaf, parsley, and one teaspoon salt. Cover with boiling water and cook slowly until tender. Remove from broth, remove skin and bones, cut meat in pieces. Parboil a sweetbread and cut in pieces. Trim kidneys, cook in broth for ten minutes, and cut in slices. Cook tongue in boiling salted water until tender. Remove skin and roots, and cut in pieces. Cut potatoes in small cubes. Mix the meats, potato, artichoke bottoms, mace, nutmeg, salt, and pepper gently together and fill the crust with the mixture. Dot with bits of butter and add enough chicken broth mixed with white wine to half fill the "coffin," as the old cook books call it. Put on top crust, make a few incisions, and bake about an hour and a quarter.

Martha Washington's recipe for this "Pie of Severall Things" calls for other ingredients which would scarcely be in keeping with the taste of today. If you would faithfully follow her, to the ingredients already given you would add cockscombs, oranges, citrons, dates, and "suckets of long bisket" (a variety of crouton), and, "if you have none of them, use gooseberries or grapes, and barberries, eyther green or pickled."

A ROYAL PASTY

- 6-pound leg of mutton
- 2 teaspoons salt
- 1/2 teaspoon ground pepper
- 1 cup chopped suet
- 3/4 teaspoon thyme
- 1 small onion
- 2 cups chopped cooked chestnuts
- 1/2 pound bacon
- 1 parboiled sweetbread
- 4 lamb kidneys, sautéd
- 4 hard-boiled eggs
- 1/2 pound mushrooms
- 1 cup artichoke bottoms
- 2 tablespoons capers
- 1 tablespoon vinegar
- 1 pint gravy or broth
- 1/2 pound butter
- Pastry

Line a large, deep dish with pastry. Remove the skin, sinews, and bones from the mutton and chop fine. Add salt, pepper, thyme, finely chopped onion, suet, chestnuts, bacon cut in small cubes, sweetbread and kidneys cut up, eggs cut in eighths, mushrooms cut in slices, artichokes, and capers. Add vinegar to the gravy or broth and moisten the mixture with this. Place in the pastry shell; dot over with butter cut in bits and lay half a dozen slices of bacon over all. Cover with a top of puff paste and bake slowly for three to four hours. The cover may be baked separately and put on the pie just before serving. Asparagus tips and half a dozen sausages cut in small pieces may be added to the pie.

A PIE OF SHEEP'S TONGUE

- 3 tongues
- 3/4 cup butter
- 1/2 cup bread crumbs
- Nutmeg
- Salt
- Pepper
- 2 tablespoon capers
- 1/2 cup white wine
- Pastry

Put tongues in a kettle, cover with boiling water, add some salt, and cook slowly until tender. Take from water, remove skin and roots, and split lengthwise. Line a dish with pastry. Lay the tongues in it and season with salt, pepper, and nutmeg. Dot over with one fourth cup butter and sprinkle bread crumbs over all. Cover with top crust and bake in moderate oven for fifty minutes. Cream the remaining butter, add the wine gradually and the capers. Lift the top crust and pour this mixture in. Serve as soon as the butter has melted.

VEAL AND BACON PIE

- 1 1/2 pounds clear veal
- 1/4 pound bacon
- 1/2 cup butter
- Yolks of 4 hard-boiled eggs
- Salt and pepper
- 1/2 teaspoon thyme
- 1/2 teaspoon marjoram
- 1/2 teaspoon winter savory
- 1 tablespoon chopped parsley
- White of 1 egg
- Pastry

Line a baking dish with pastry. Cut veal in small cubes and place in the dish. Cut bacon in small pieces, fry until nearly done, and add. Season all with salt and pepper. Mash the egg yolks and add thyme, marjoram, savory, parsley, salt, and pepper. Bind with egg white and form into small balls. Lay on the meat, dot over with butter, put on the top crust, and bake in a slow oven one and a half hours.

VEAL PIE

2	pounds clear veal, cooked		Salt
			Pepper
1/2	cup butter		Nutmeg
2	tablespoons capers	1/2	lemon, sliced
6	hard-boiled eggs	2	dozen oysters
1	cup gravy		Pastry

Line a deep, round dish with pastry. Dot over with half the butter, one tablespoon of capers, and half the oysters, cut up. Cut the veal in small pieces. Mix the gravy, salt, pepper, and nutmeg, and put in the pie. Add remaining butter in small bits, oysters, another tablespoon of capers, and the lemon, cut in very thin slices, then in quarters. Add top crust and bake one hour in a medium oven.

PORK PIE

2	pounds fresh ham		Pepper
	Cloves	1/2	cup butter
	Mace		Claret or white wine
	Salt		Pastry

Have the butcher lard the meat with bacon. Rub it over well with salt, pepper, cloves, and mace. Place in a dish and cover with the wine. Let soak for two days, turning several times. Line a dish with pastry. Remove pork from wine, dry with a piece of linen, and cut it in small pieces. Roll in a little flour. Put into the pastry shell and season with salt and pepper. Add some of the wine in which the meat has soaked, about one cupful; cover with top crust, and bake in a slow oven two hours.

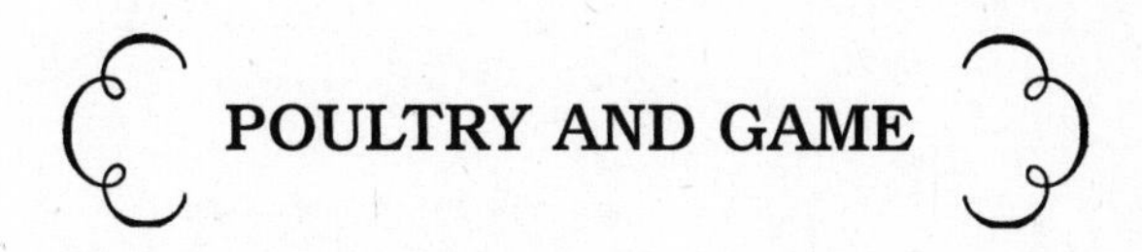

POULTRY AND GAME

MOUNT VERNON LOOKING EAST

POULTRY AND GAME

ROAST CAPON WITH OYSTERS

1 capon
2 1/2 cups bread crumbs
Salt and pepper
1 white onion
1 pint oysters
2/3 cup claret
1 teaspoon vinegar
4 tablespoons butter
1 tablespoon flour
3/4 cup boiling water
1 tablespoon lemon rind
Sliced lemon

Dress the capon. Rub over with salt and pepper and some butter. Mix the bread crumbs with the butter, and salt and pepper, half of the onion cut up very fine, and the oysters which have been cleaned. Stuff the capon with this mixture and put in a hot oven. As the capon browns, baste often with two tablespoons butter melted in boiling water. When tender, remove to hot platter and make gravy as follows: To essence in pan, add claret, vinegar, a grating of pepper, lemon rind, and flour mixed with remaining two tablespoons butter. Decorate capon with sliced lemon and pour gravy around it.

CAPON AFTER THE FLANDERS' FASHION

1	capon	1	marrow bone
1	quart white wine		Salt
1	quart boiling water		Pepper-corns
1	pint mutton broth		Whole mace
	Parsley	1/2	teaspoon sugar
4	carrots		Toast points

Dress the capon, tie in a cheesecloth, and place in kettle. Pour over it boiling water, wine, and mutton broth (this may be omitted). Cut the carrots in pieces and add, together with the marrow bone, whole mace, sugar, salt to taste, and a few pepper-corns. Boil until tender. Place on hot platter, decorated with parsley and toast points, and serve with Sauce for a Capon.

TO STEW A DUCK THE FRENCH WAY

1	duck	1	blade of mace
	Salt		Few pepper-corns
	Sprig of thyme	3/4	cup water
	Spring of marjoram	1 1/2	cups claret
	Sprig of winter savory	2	tablespoons butter
	Sprig of rosemary		Yolks of 5 eggs
1	onion		

Clean and wash the duck. Rub over with salt and put in a hot oven. Roast until a delicate brown. Remove duck from the oven and cut it up. Place in a stew pan with water, claret, spices, and onion, cut in half. Stew gently until the meat is tender. Remove to a hot platter. Add the butter to the gravy and stir in well-beaten egg yolks. Pour over the duck and serve.

TO BOIL PIGEONS

	Pigeons or squabs	1	tablespoon chopped parsley
1	whole mace	2	tablespoons capers
1/2	teaspoon whole cloves	1	cup butter
	Salt		Stock
1/4	teaspoon pepper-corns		Toast points

Allow one pigeon or squab for each person. Plunge four pigeons, or squabs, which have been dressed and trussed, into a kettle of boiling water. Parboil for half an hour. Remove, put in another pan, and nearly cover with strong stock. Add mace, cloves, pepper-corns, one half cup butter, and parsley. Simmer until tender; it will take about three hours. Remove from pan, drain, place on pieces of toast, and pour over them remaining one half cup butter melted, and browned, to which capers have been added.

PIGEON PIE

4	pigeons		Pepper and salt
1/4	pound bacon		Butter
6	sausages	2	tablespoons white wine
			Pastry

Disjoint and bone the pigeons. Rub over with salt and pepper. Line a deep, round dish with pastry. Dot with butter, and put in the pigeons. Dice the bacon and cut the sausages in small pieces, add to the pie. Dot over with more butter and put on the top crust, slashing it here and there. Bake in a medium oven for two hours. When done, cream three tablespoons of butter with the white wine. Lift the top crust and add this mixture.

PIGEONS WITH PUDDING

6 pigeons
Celery
1 cup bread crumbs
3 eggs
1/2 cup cream
1/4 cup chopped suet
1/4 cup white wine
Grated mace
Grated nutmeg
Cinnamon
1/4 teaspoon sweet marjoram
1/4 teaspoon tarragon
2 tablespoons dried currants

Clean and dress the pigeons. Drop into boiling salted water, which contains a few stalks of celery. Cover and let simmer until tender. Meanwhile make the puddings or force-meat. Cook the bread crumbs and cream to a paste. Add suet, wine, and eggs, well beaten. Season with salt, a dash each of mace, nutmeg, and cinnamon, sweet marjoram, tarragon, and dried currants. The mixture should be stiff. Shape in the form of eggs. Take small pieces of linen or cheesecloth, dust with flour, and tie the puddings in them. Drop into the pot with the pigeons and boil for half an hour. Remove pigeons to platter, put a piece of rosemary on each breast, and "betwixt every pigeon, a pudding," from which the cloth has, of course, been removed. Pour Sauce for Pigeons over them.

TO STEW SPARROWS

6 or 8 sparrows
Salt
1/2 teaspoon rosemary
1/2 teaspoon sweet marjoram
1 cup white wine
3/4 cup veal broth
Stick of cinnamon
Whole mace
2 tablespoons dried currants
1/2 teaspoon sugar
4 dates

The number of sparrows will depend upon your huntsman. We will suppose there are six or eight.

Dress sparrows and plunge them in boiling salted water, to which has been added rosemary and marjoram. Boil for twenty minutes. In another pan put the white wine and veal broth, cinnamon, mace, currants, dates, cut up, and sugar. Let come to a boil. Add the sparrows and simmer gently until tender. The sauce may be thickened with one tablespoon soft butter mixed with one tablespoon flour. Add more salt if necessary.

TO ROAST A HARE

1	hare	4	strips of bacon
	Large sprig of parsley	4	hard-boiled eggs
	Sprig of marjoram	1/2	cup butter
	Sprig of thyme	1	tablespoon vinegar
	Salt and pepper	2	tablespoons currants

3/4 cup stock

Dress the hare and rub over with salt and pepper. Lay strips of bacon across the breast. Chop the eggs, and add thyme, chopped parsley, marjoram, salt, and pepper. Fill the cavity of the hare with this mixture. Put in hot oven, surrounded by stock. Bake about one hour, basting often. When tender, cut off meat from bones and cut in small pieces. "Mingle with it that which was in the bellie," adding butter, vinegar, currants, and gravy from pan. The original recipe directs "soe let you heat ym together. Serve it up in a faire dish, ye bones lying about it, & ye back bone in ye midst." For the taste of today, the bones may delicately be omitted.

CHICKEN PIE

1	chicken		Mace
1 1/2	pounds forequarter of lamb		Butter
		1	tablespoon flour
1	small onion		Grated nutmeg
	Stalk of celery		Salt
	Bay leaf		Pepper-corns
	Whole cloves	3/4	cup white wine
6	hard-boiled eggs		Lemon juice

Pastry

Disjoint the chicken and place in a stewing pan, together with the onion, bay leaf, celery, cloves, salt, and pepper-corns. Cover with boiling water and cook gently until tender. Cut lamb into small pieces, remove any skin or fat, roll in flour seasoned with pepper and salt, brown in a little butter, add boiling water half to cover, and stew until tender. Remove chicken from the stock; remove bones and skin and cut in pieces. Line a deep, round dish with pastry. Lay in it the pieces of chicken, lamb, artichoke bottoms, and hard-boiled eggs cut in quarters. Sprinkle with salt, pepper, grated nutmeg, and a little mace, and dot over thickly with butter. Then take one and a quarter cups chicken stock, and add three quarter cup white wine and, if desired, some lemon juice. Thicken with a flour mixed with a tablespoon butter and pour into the pie. Put on top crust, slash, and bake in a moderate oven one hour.

If you have a sweet tooth, Martha Washington advises adding shredded dates, sugar, citron, raisins, currants, and candied lettuce stalks.

SAUCES

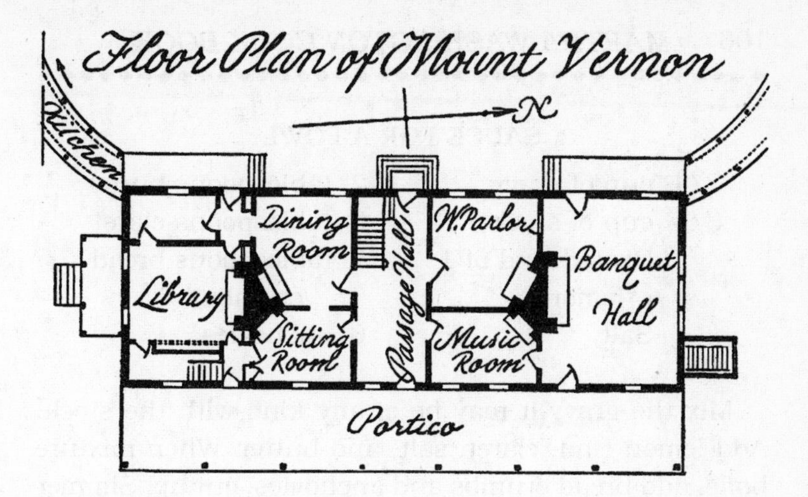

SAUCES

The fine Italian hand of the French chef is not yet discernible in the sauces for meat and fish that have come down to us in Martha Washington's Cook Book. These sauces are simple and direct, no nonsense about them. Often only the broth in which the meat or fish was boiled is used as a sauce. In two or three cases a modern sauce has been suggested as making a dish more palatable. They are indicated as such.

SAUCE FOR A HEN

1 cup lamb gravy
2 hard-boiled eggs
1/2 teaspoon mustard
Juice of 1 lemon

Heat the gravy. Add finely chopped eggs, mustard, and lemon juice. Simmer two or three minutes and serve.

SAUCE FOR A FOWL

- 3/4 cup of gravy
- 3/4 cup of stock
- Grated rind of 1 lemon
- Salt
- 2 tablespoons butter
- 3 tablespoons claret
- 2 tablespoons bread crumbs
- 6 anchovies

Mix the gravy-it may be of any kind-with the stock. Add lemon rind, claret, salt, and butter. When mixture boils, add bread crumbs and anchovies, cut up. Simmer for five minutes.

SAUCE FOR A CAPON

- 1 dozen large oysters
- 3/4 cup claret
- 2 tablespoons butter
- 1 small white onion
- Whole mace
- 1 teaspoon grated lemon rind
- Salt
- 2 tablespoons very fine bread crumbs

Melt two tablespoons butter, add onion cut up fine, and fry a delicate gold. Add claret, mace, lemon rind, and salt. Simmer for ten minutes. Add the oysters and their liquor, and thicken with bread crumbs. Add another piece of butter, as large as you will, and serve.

SAUCE FOR PIGEONS

- 3/4 cup white wine
- 2 tablespoons butter
- 1/2 teaspoon vinegar
- 1/2 teaspoon sugar
- Salt and pepper
- Yolks of 2 eggs

Bring the wine to a boil, add the butter, vinegar, sugar, salt, and pepper, and simmer a few minutes. Beat the yolks of the eggs and add gradually to first mixture. Do not allow to boil.

BREAD SAUCE

2	cups milk	1	teaspoon vinegar
1/2	cup fine bread crumbs		Grating of nutmeg
1	small onion	1/4	cup butter
6	whole cloves	1/2	teaspoon sugar

Salt

Heat the milk in a double boiler with the bread crumbs and onion stuck with cloves. Cook half an hour. Add vinegar, sugar, nutmeg, butter and a little salt if needed. Remove onion before serving.

SAUCE FOR HADDOCK

1/3	cup butter	1	tablespoon lemon juice
2	tablespoons flour	1	tablespoon capers
1/3	cup fish stock	2	anchovies
1	cup white wine		

Salt and pepper

Melt the butter and add flour gradually. When thoroughly blended stir in the fish stock, wine and lemon juice. Season to taste with salt and pepper. Add anchovies, crushed to a paste, and capers.

SAUCE FOR CARP

- 2 cups white wine
- 1/2 cup currants
- 1 blade of mace
- Bunch of sweet herbs
- 2 tablespoons butter
- 1 teaspoon sugar
- Salt

Combine the above ingredients and boil slowly for twenty minutes. Pour over the fish.

SAUCE FOR BOILED LAMB OR MUTTON

- 2 tablespoons butter
- 2 scant tablespoons flour
- Lamb or mutton broth
- 1/2 tablespoon vinegar
- 1/2 teaspoon sugar
- 1 tablespoon chopped parsley

Melt the butter and add the flour gradually. Let bubble up well. Gradually stir about one cup of broth, according to consistency desired. Add vinegar, sugar and chopped parsley.

MAÎTRE D'HÔTEL BUTTER (MODERN)

- 4 tablespoons sweet butter
- 3/4 tablespoon lemon juice
- 1/4 teaspoon salt
- 1/8 teaspoon black pepper
- 1 teaspoon finely chopped parsley

Cream the butter with a wooden spoon until light and fluffy. Add salt, freshly ground pepper, and lemon juice, drop by drop, so as to avoid curdling. Finally add parsley.

CAPER SAUCE (MODERN)

- 1/4 cup butter
- 2 tablespoons flour
- 1/8 teaspoon salt
- 1/8 teaspoon white pepper
- 1 cup hot water
- 1 teaspoon lemon juice
- 3 tablespoons capers
- 1 tablespoon butter

Melt the quarter cup of butter and gradually stir in the flour, mixed with the salt and pepper. Slowly add boiling water and simmer three minutes. Add the capers and, bit by bit, one tablespoon of butter.

MUSTARD SAUCE (MODERN)

- 2 tablespoons butter
- 1 1/2 tablespoons flour
- 1 cup hot water
- 1/4 teaspoon salt
- 1/8 teaspoon pepper
- 1 teaspoon lemon juice
- 1 teaspoon prepared mustard
- Yolks of two eggs
- Additional butter

Melt the butter, add flour and let bubble over a low fire until thoroughly blended. Add salt and pepper and, very gradually, hot water. Simmer for two minutes while stirring constantly. Add lemon juice and mustard and, just before serving, stir in the well-beaten egg yolks. Do not boil after this.

TOMATO SAUCE (MODERN)

- 2 tablespoons butter
- 1 tablespoon flour
- 1/2 small white onion
- 1 cup tomato purée
- 1/8 teaspoon ground nutmeg
- 1 teaspoon sugar
- 1/2 teaspoon salt
- 1/8 teaspoon black pepper

Chop the onion very fine. Melt the butter and cook the onion in it very slowly until a golden brown. Add the flour, spices, and lastly the tomato purée. Boil slowly for two minutes until smooth.

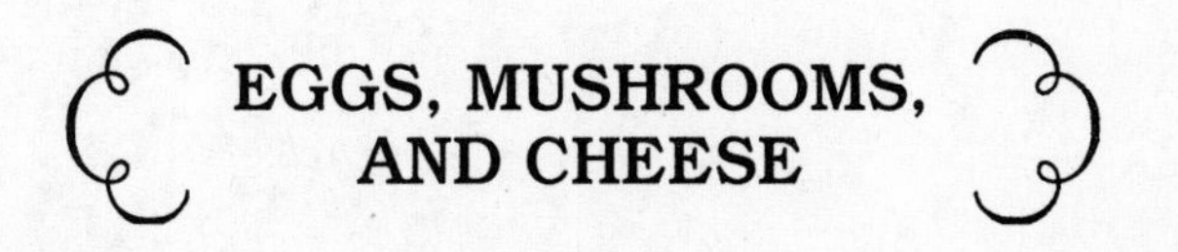

EGGS, MUSHROOMS, AND CHEESE

THE OLD BARN, MOUNT VERNON

EGGS, MUSHROOMS, AND CHEESE

Eggs, to all intents and purposes, are ignored in the *Cook Book*. Doubtless they appeared as usual at the breakfast table, and no plantation cook needed directions for scrambling them or for producing a large platter of "sunny sides up," with ribbons of crisp and transparent bacon. "Buttered eggs" were a *spécialité de la maison*, and were thus duly set down.

Vegetables are treated in the same cavalier manner. With the exception of "A Tart of Parsnips," "A Lettice Tart," and directions for dressing "A dish of Mushrumps," there are no recipes for the preparation of vegetables. In all the accounts of dinners at Mount Vernon left, as a rule, by men as the chief "writing folk" of the day, attention is focused on the meats and other stout articles of diet, with vegetables, as usual, accepted as a necessary evil.

Whether "Uncle Harkless," the cook, sent his "snaps" and "greens" to table cooked in the old Virginia fashion with a piece of pork or bacon, or whether Mrs. Washington had taught him to "dress" his vegetables after the manner of English cooks, has not been recorded. Other cook books of the day, such as *The Compleat Housewife,* give directions for dressing greens and roots, spinach, carrots, potatoes, turnips, asparagus, French beans, artichokes, "colleflowers," and "brockala"–all prepared and served very much as they would be now.

TO MAKE CURDS

1 quart whole milk	Salt
1 pint cream	2 tablespoons sugar

Set milk, with salt, on the fire and bring slowly to boil; then add half a cup of cream. Do this four times, until all the cream is used. Turn into a flat dish and set overnight in a cool place. Skim off the top, put in a glass plate, dust with sugar, and serve. A little grated nutmeg or a little cinnamon adds to the flavor.

CURDS, ANOTHER WAY

3 cups cream	Sugar
7 eggs	Salt
Seasonings	

Beat the eggs well, stir in the cream, and cook in a double boiler until very thick. Season to taste when cold, with sugar, salt, and whatever spices you wish.

MUSHROOMS IN CREAM

1 pound mushrooms	Salt and pepper
1 small white onion	1 tablespoon chopped parsley
3/4 cup heavy cream	
Pinch of thyme	Grated nutmeg
2 tablespoons butter	

Wash and peel the mushrooms; then cut in slices, lengthwise. Add the onion, cut in half, and set over a slow fire. Stew gently for ten minutes, discarding any water that may rise. Remove the onion and add thyme, nutmeg, parsley, cream, and salt and pepper to taste. Cook for five minutes, stirring often. Add butter and serve. The addition, at the last moment, of the yolks of two eggs is an improvement.

FRESH ALMOND CHEESE

1 cup blanched almonds
1 cup water
Pinch of salt
3 tablespoons sugar
Juice of 1 orange
Juice of 1 lemon
Cinnamon

Grind the almonds very fine. Add water, sugar, salt, and fruit juices. Set on the stove and cook for ten minutes. Cool for fifteen minutes. Drain through several thicknesses of cheesecloth, letting it stand for several hours. Remove from cloth, form into a round, dust with sugar and cinnamon, and surround with cream.

FRESH CHEESE WITH ALMONDS

1 cup cottage cheese
1/2 pound almonds
2 tablespoons rose water
1/2 cup sugar
1/2 cup currants
1/8 teaspoon salt
Sugar and cream

Blanch, chop, and pound the almonds with the rose water until a smooth mass. Add the cottage cheese, sugar, and salt, and beat well. Add the currants, which have soaked in rose water for an hour. Press into a mould and let stand several hours. Turn out, surround with cream, sweetened and flavored with rose water to taste.

BUTTERED EGGS

6 eggs
2 anchovies
1/2 cup lamb gravy
1/4 teaspoon salt
Pepper
1 large tablespoon butter
Grated nutmeg

Crush the anchovies with a fork and add to gravy. Beat the eggs slightly with a silver fork and add gravy to them, with salt and some freshly ground black pepper. Melt butter in skillet and add eggs. Scramble over a slow fire. Turn on to a hot platter and grate some nutmeg over the top.

FRENCH CURDS

Whites of 5 eggs
Yolks of 2 eggs
1 pint cream
Rosemary
1/2 grated nutmeg
2 tablespoons rose water
2 tablespoons orange juice
2 tablespoons lemon juice
Salt
Sugar

Beat the eggs together until light. Add the cream and strain into a saucepan. Add rose water and nutmeg. Set on the fire and stir constantly until mixture thickens. Add lemon and orange juice. Stir until it curdles. Turn into a fine cheesecloth and hang up, so that the whey may run from it. Let hang for an hour. Season the curds to taste with sugar and a dash of salt. Serve with the following sauce.

SAUCE FOR FRENCH CURDS

Yolks of 2 eggs
2 tablespoons sugar
1/4 cup rose water

Beat egg yolks until light together with sugar and rose water. "If you please, you may put in some white wine."

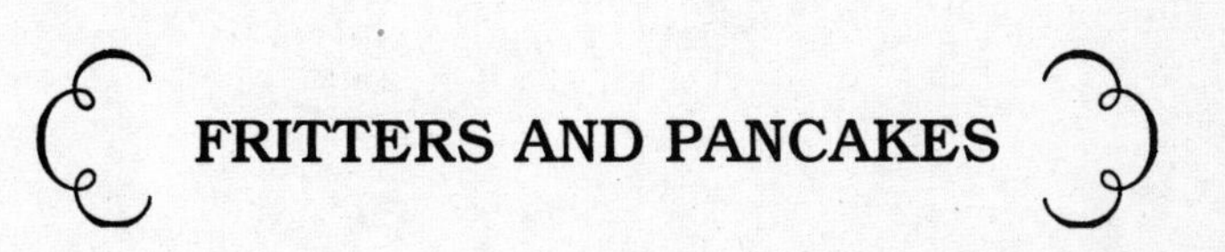

FRITTERS AND PANCAKES

THE MARTHA WASHINGTON KITCHEN, WILLIAMSBURG, VA.

FRITTERS AND PANCAKES

APPLE FRITTERS

1	cup ale	1/4	teaspoon nutmeg
1/4	cup white wine	1/4	teaspoon cloves
	Yolks of 4 eggs	1/4	teaspoon mace
	White of 1 egg		Apples
1	cup flour		Sugar
1/4	teaspoon salt		Cinnamon

Heat the ale, add wine and eggs, well beaten. Mix the spices with the flour and combine the two mixtures. As our author says: "Your batter must be no thicker than will just hang on the apples." A little more or less flour may be needed. Cut the apples in rounds, or whatever shape you please, and dip in the batter. Drop in deep fat and fry a golden brown. Drain on a piece of clean linen, sprinkle with sugar and cinnamon, and serve.

FRENCH FRITTERS

1 cup flour
1/2 cup cottage cheese
3 eggs
2 tablespoons marrow, chopped fine
1 tablespoon candied lemon peel, chopped fine
1/2 cup sugar
1/2 cup white wine
1/8 teaspoon salt
3 small apples, chopped fine
Butter
Cinnamon

Sift the flour together with salt and sugar. Add cottage cheese, marrow, and well-beaten eggs mixed with white wine. Stir in the lemon peel and apples. Melt some butter in a skillet and drop in the batter in lumps the size of a walnut. Fry to a golden brown on each side. Dust with cinnamon and sugar before serving. Butter may be substituted for the marrow.

FRITTERS, ANOTHER WAY

Whites of 3 eggs
3 tablespoons rose water
1/4 teaspoon cloves and cinnamon
1/4 teaspoon salt
1 pint milk
1 cup flour
3 or 4 apples, depending on size
Butter
Cinnamon
Sugar

Sift the flour into a bowl together with the salt and spices. Pour the milk on gradually, until a smooth batter is formed. Beat the egg whites until very light and fold into the batter. Add rosewater. Cut apples in small, thin slivers. Dust with flour and fold in the batter. Melt some butter in a frying pan. Drop in the fritter batter by the spoonful, fry slowly until a golden brown on both sides. Sprinkle with cinnamon and sugar, and serve.

TO MAKE PANCAKES

- 1 1/2 cups cream
- 3 eggs
- 1/2 cup flour
- 2/3 cup fine bread crumbs
- 2 tablespoons rose water
- 1/4 teaspoon salt
- Spices
- Butter

Scald the cream and pour over the bread crumbs. Let stand half an hour. Add flour, well-beaten eggs, salt, and rose water. Add spices to taste. The batter should be thin. Fry in butter.

TO MAKE PANCAKES ANOTHER WAY

- 2 cups ale
- 1/2 cup white wine
- 2 tablespoons rose water
- 3 eggs
- 1/2 teaspoon grated nutmeg
- 1 cup flour
- 1/4 teaspoon salt
- Butter
- Cinnamon
- Sugar

Warm the ale. Beat the eggs well and combine. Add wine and rose water. Sift together salt, nutmeg, and flour, and gradually pour onto it the first mixture. Stir until a smooth mass. The dough and the resulting pancakes should be very thin. Fry in butter, and serve with cinnamon and sugar.

FRIED APPLE CAKES

	Baked apples, about 5	Butter
3	tablespoons flour	Sugar
4	eggs	Rose water
1/4	teaspoon salt	Candied lemon peel

Peel and bake sour apples as usual, then mash them. There should be one cupful of the pulp. To this, add the well-beaten eggs, salt, and flour. Melt some butter in a skillet and fry the mixture in small cakes, about two inches across. When brown on one side, turn and brown on the other. Remove to a hot platter and garnish each cake with three or four wedges of candied lemon peel. Sprinkle with sugar and a little rose water.

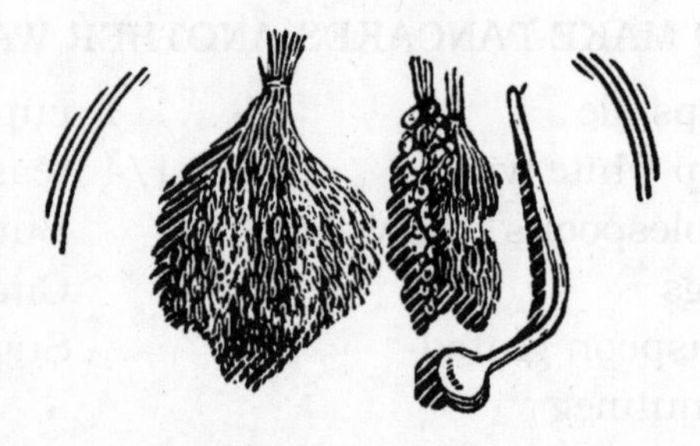

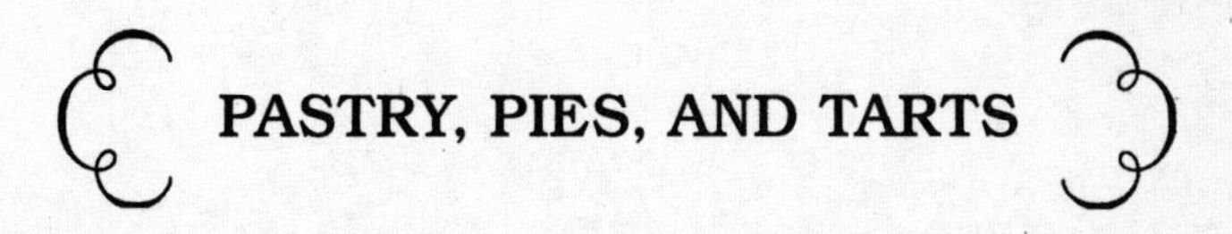

PASTRY, PIES, AND TARTS

THE KITCHEN FIREPLACE, MOUNT VERNON

PASTRY, PIES, AND TARTS

The earliest English cook books abound with recipes for pies of every description, from pies of larks to tarts of gooseberries. American cooks carried on this tradition; indeed, they transformed the very meaning of the word "pie." Whereas in English cookery it had hitherto applied primarily to meat pies, in America the word was extended to include sweet pies, and the expression "tart" was gradually abandoned in common use. At Mount Vernon, pies of veal, pork, sheep tongues, or "of severall things" were served. Martha Washington proved herself a real American by using pie and tart interchangeably for sweet concoctions.

PUFF PASTE

1	pound flour	1/4	teaspoon salt
1 1/4	pounds butter		Whites of 4 eggs
	Water		

Wash the butter thoroughly and shape into a long roll. Set in the refrigerator for an hour or two. Sift flour and salt into a bowl. Form a hole in the center and pour in the egg whites. Stir around and around, in a circular motion. Do not knead. Add a little cold water, if necessary, to form a paste. Roll out until very thin. Place the butter in the center and fold the dough over from four sides. Put in refrigerator for fifteen minutes. Roll lengthwise until blisters of butter appear. Fold bottom and top to center and roll crosswise. Fold again from bottom and then from top, and roll once more. Place on ice for twenty minutes. Repeat procedure. Place in refrigerator again and repeat once more.

QUICK PUFF PASTE

1	quart flour	1/4	teaspoon salt
	Yolks of 3 eggs	1/4	cup milk or more
	Whites of 5 eggs	1/2	pound butter

Sift together the flour and salt. Beat the eggs, add milk, and stir into the flour to form a stiff paste. A little more milk may be needed, depending on the flour used. Roll into a thin sheet and dot with pieces of butter. Sift a little flour over this, fold, and roll out again. Do this four times. Chill thoroughly before using.

ROYAL PASTE

1	quart flour	2	tablespoons sugar
3	eggs	1	tablespoon rose water
1/2	pound butter	1	cup white wine

Water

Sift together the flour, sugar, and salt. Cut the butter in small pieces and work into flour. Beat the eggs well; add rose water and wine, and stir into the first mixture to form a stiff paste. A little water may be added if needed. "But take heed to be not made too stiff, nor worke it over much, nor heat it with yr hand."

A CUSTARD PIE

2	cups cream		Yolks of 4 eggs
	Piece of a whole nutmeg		Whites of 2 eggs
	Piece of stick cinnamon	2	tablespoons white wine
1/4	small bay leaf	3	tablespoons sugar
	Salt	2	tablespoons rose water

1/2 cup almonds

Scald the cream with the nutmeg, cinnamon, and bay leaf, and set aside to cool a little. Beat the eggs well, together with the wine, sugar, and a pinch of salt. Combine the two mixtures. Pound the almonds well in a mortar and mix with rose water. Have ready a pie dish lined with pastry. Strew the crushed almonds in this, add the custard mixture, and bake in a moderate oven until set.

APPLE PUFFS

6 apples	3 whole cloves
3/4 cup red wine	1 teaspoon lemon peel, cut fine
3/4 cup sugar	1 teaspoon orange peel, cut fine
1/8 teaspoon grated nutmeg	

Pastry

Pare the apples and cut in quarters. Mix the wine, sugar, and spices, lemon and orange peel, and bring to a boil. Add the apples and stew slowly until clear and tender. Roll out the pastry and cut in squares of about four inches. Place a large spoonful of the apples in the middle. Bring the corners of the pastry together at the top and press the "edges." Place on a buttered sheet and bake in a moderate oven until a light brown. Any remaining juice in which the apples were stewed may be used as sauce. More wine and sugar may be added if needed.

TO MAKE MINCED PIES

2 pounds beef	1/2 tablespoon cinnamon
2 pounds veal	1/2 tablespoon cloves
2 pounds suet	1/2 tablespoon mace
2 cups broth	1/2 tablespoon nutmeg
1 pound raisins	1/2 pound citron
1 1/2 pounds currants	1/2 pound lemon peel
6 apples	1/2 pound orange peel
1/4 cup rose water	Salt
1 3/4 cups sugar	1 cup white wine

Cover the meat and suet with boiling water and cook slowly until tender. Let cool. Remove the crust of suet that has formed and crumble it fine. Chop the meat very fine. Add suet, apples chopped fine, currants, chopped raisins, citron, lemon, and orange peel, in fine pieces, sugar, and salt to taste. Add broth, bring all to a boil, and let cook slowly for one and a half hours. Add rose water, wine, and spices. "For plaine minced pies, leave out ye fruit and put in blanchd almonds minced small."

A TART OF HIPPS[1]

1 quart hipps	Cinnamon
White wine	Ginger
Sugar	Salt
Rose water	2 eggs

Gather a quart of hipps. Wash hipps, cut in two, and remove the kernels. Cover with white wine and let soak an hour or two. Set on the stove and cook until tender. Drain off the wine in which they cooked and press the hipps through a strainer. It should be a fairly thick mass. Season to taste with sugar, rose water, and a dash each of cinnamon, ginger, and salt. Add eggs well beaten. Pour into a pie plate lined with pastry and place in a moderate oven to bake until set.

[1] A tart of hipps would be, at the very least, unusual today, if not impracticable. It would seem to demand a rose garden to start with, for the "hipps" are not what we usually associate with that word but the fruit of the rose, more particularly the dog rose. For those hardy souls who would like to experiment, here is the recipe.

TO MAKE A LETTUCE TART

4	heads romaine lettuce	Cinnamon
		Ginger
1 1/2	dozen large prunes	Butter
	Sugar	Marrow
	Salt	Pastry

Line a deep pie dish with pastry. Dot over with bits of butter, and sprinkle with sugar, a little cinnamon, and ginger. Cook the romaine in boiling, salted water until tender. Drain and lay in the pastry. On top of this lay the prunes, which have been soaked, pitted, and cooked until tender. Dot over with cubes of marrow, a little sugar, and cinnamon. Cover with the upper crust and bake about three-quarters of an hour. For those who do not share Martha Washington's sweet tooth, the sugar and spices may be omitted.

A TART OF PARSNIPS

8	young parsnips		Sugar
	White wine		Juice of 1 lemon
3	eggs		Rose water
1/2	cup grated bread crumbs	2	tablespoons butter
			Pastry

Wash and peel the parsnips; be sure they are young. Cut in pieces and cook until tender in half white wine, half water. Drain well and pound to a pulp in a mortar. Add the beaten eggs, grated bread, and season with rose water and white wine. Force through a strainer, add sugar to taste, the lemon juice, and the butter melted. Turn into a pie plate lined with pastry and bake until set. "Ye juice of leamons you may eyther put in or leave out at yr pleasure."

QUINCE PIE

8 quinces	1 1/2 cups water
1 1/4 cup sugar	Pastry

Wash the quinces. Cut in quarters, remove cores, and peel. Put in a pan together with one cup sugar and water, and let stew very slowly until tender. Turn fruit often. Line a pie plate with pastry and arrange the quinces in it in a neat design. Pour on the syrup and sprinkle with remaining one-fourth cup sugar. Lay criss-cross pieces of pastry on top and bake until a golden brown. The top pastry may be omitted and the pie covered with whipped cream before serving. Martha Washington did not do this.

PUFF KIDS

1 quart flour	1 pound butter
Whites of 3 eggs	1/4 teaspoon salt
Yolks of 3 eggs	Milk

Sift together the flour and salt. Beat the eggs until light and stir into the flour. Add the butter, cut up in small bits, and enough milk to form a stiff paste. Beat and work it until a smooth paste is formed. "Use this paste," says Martha Washington, "for pasties, dishes or patty pan.

MARROW PIE

- 1/4 pound beef marrow
- 1 veal kidney
- 1 veal tongue
- Yolks of 3 eggs
- 1 cup sugar
- 1/2 teaspoon salt
- 3 tablespoons rose water
- 1 cup currants
- 1 cup raisins
- 2 tablespoons lemon peel, chopped
- 2 tablespoons cream
- 2 tablespoons bread crumbs
- 6 macaroons, crumbled
- Pastry

Chop the marrow, kidney, and tongue very fine. Add the other ingredients in the order given. Line a pie plate with pastry, fill with the mixture, and cover with upper crust. Bake in a moderate oven. This is on the order of mince pie.

A CODDLING TART

- 4 apples
- 1 cup sugar
- 2/3 cup water
- Pastry
- Heavy cream

Peel and core the apples, cut in half crosswise. Boil three-quarters cup sugar with water for five minutes. Add apples and cook slowly until tender, turning several times. If the syrup gets too thick, a spoonful of water may be added. Line a pie dish with pastry and place the apples side by side in this. Pour over them the syrup and dust with remaining sugar. Set in a moderate oven until the pastry is a golden brown. Serve cold with "as you pleas, a little thick, sweet cream." For variation, the syrup in which the apples are cooked may be colored with red or green vegetable color paste, which will tint the apples.

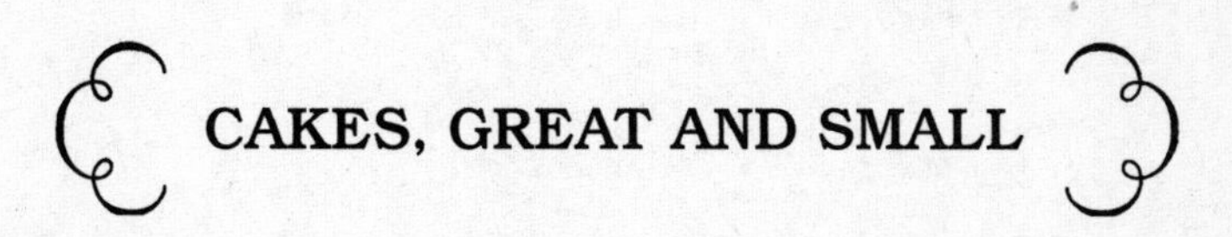

CAKES, GREAT AND SMALL

CAKES, GREAT AND SMALL

There were always cakes in abundance at Mount Vernon. Fruit cakes were the most popular, heavy with spices, and rich with "currans and raisins of ye sun." Long known as a "great cake" or an "excellent cake," fruit cake was not so called until Victorian days. To us a "great cake" seems well named, as we read the appalling directions to "take a peck of floure and put to it ten eggs and mingle with ye floure two pound of fresh butter." For state occasions there were likely to be "Maids of Honour.... Mackroons," or perhaps "Marchpane," a concoction of almond and sugar which the cook was directed to "beat together the space of an hour." Christmas called for "Shrewsbury cakes," "Jumballs" of varying sorts, as well as "Cullerd Gingerbread." The layer cake as we know it did not exist.

The baking of cakes at Mount Vernon differed greatly

from our present American way. There was, of course, no baking powder, and the lightness of the cake depended on the thoroughness of the beating, a method which persists in Europe today. No French cook uses baking powder; it is even doubtful whether she has ever heard of it. The batter is vigorously belabored with a wire whisk, put in the pan, shaken down, and set in the oven. It rises to a golden crown quite as well as if it contained the traditional "two heaping teaspoonsful of baking powder," and the texture is much more delicate and firm.

SUGAR CAKES

4 cups flour
1/2 cup sugar
Yolks of 2 eggs
1/2 teaspoon salt
4 tablespoons cream
1 1/2 cups butter
1 tablespoon rose water

Sift the flour into a bowl in the shape of a cone. Make a hole in the center of the cone, like a crater. Into this put the sugar, the yolks of eggs beaten with the cream and rose water. Break the butter in small pieces and dot around the edges of the flour. Work all together with the hands, mixing and kneading it thoroughly. Roll out, cut in circles, place on buttered pan, dust with sugar, and bake until a pale brown.

SUGAR CAKES, ANOTHER WAY

4 cups flour
1 cup sugar
1/4 teaspoon salt
Yolk of 1 egg
1 tablespoon wine
1 tablespoon rose water
1 1/2 cups melted butter

Sift together flour, sugar, and salt. Mix the wine, rose water, and melted butter, and work into the first mixture until a smooth paste is formed. Roll very thin and cut, says Martha Washington, with a beer glass. Place on buttered sheets and bake.

SUGAR CAKES, STILL ANOTHER WAY

4 cups flour
2 cups sugar
1 teaspoon cinnamon
3/4 pound butter
Whites of 4 eggs
2/3 cup white wine
1/2 teaspoon salt

Sift together the flour, salt, sugar, and cinnamon. Work the butter into the mixture with the tips of the fingers. Beat the eggs slightly and add white wine. Mingle all together until it forms a paste that can be rolled out. A little more wine may be needed. Roll thin, cut in fancy shapes, and bake in a moderate oven.

CARAWAY CAKES

1 pound flour
1 pound butter
3 eggs
1 cup sugar
3 tablespoons cream
2 teaspoons baking powder
1/2 teaspoon salt
3/4 cup caraway seeds

Sift together the flour, sugar, salt, and baking powder. Work in the butter with the finger tips. Add caraway seeds. Moisten with the eggs, well beaten and mixed with the cream. More cream may be added if needed. Roll Out, shape into cakes, and bake in a moderate oven.

ANISEED CAKES

4 cups flour	3/4 cup aniseed
1 cup sugar	2 cups butter
1/2 teaspoon salt	2 eggs

Sift together flour, salt, and sugar. Add aniseed, work in the melted butter and eggs to form a dough. Roll out, cut into shapes, and bake in a moderate oven.

SHREWSBURY CAKES

1 quart flour	1/2 teaspoon cloves
3/4 pound butter	1/2 teaspoon mace
1 cup sugar	Whites of 2 eggs
1/2 teaspoon salt	1/2 cup rose water
1 teaspoon cinnamon	1/2 cup white wine

Warm cream

Sift together flour, sugar, salt, and spices. Work in the butter with the finger tips. Beat the eggs slightly, and add rose water and wine. Blend with first mixture, adding enough warm cream to form a soft dough. Roll out, cut into fancy shapes, and bake in a moderate oven.

SHREWSBURY CAKES, ANOTHER WAY

1 pound sugar	1/2 teaspoon nutmeg
1 pound flour	1/2 teaspoon ginger
1 teaspoon cinnamon	2 eggs
1/2 teaspoon salt	Melted butter

Sift together the flour, sugar, salt, and spices. Add the beaten eggs and enough melted butter to make a paste, at least one cupful. Roll about half an inch thick. Cut in rounds, place on a buttered sheet, and bake in a moderate oven.

EXCELLENT CURRANT CAKES

1	pound butter	1	pound currants
1	pound flour	3	eggs
1	pound sugar	1/2	teaspoon salt

Rose water

Wash the butter well in rose water. Sift together the flour, sugar, and salt. Cream the butter well and mix with the flour and sugar. Add currants, well-beaten eggs, and enough rose water to form a stiff dough. Divide into pans and bake. The lightness of the cake depends on the thoroughness with which the dough is beaten.

JUMBLES

3/4	cup butter	6	tablespoons rose water
1 1/2	cups sugar	1/2	teaspoon salt
	Yolks of 6 eggs	1	tablespoon caraway seeds
	Whites of 3 eggs		
6	tablespoons cream		

Cream the butter well. Add sugar gradually, well-beaten eggs, cream, rose water, caraway seeds, and enough flour sifted with the salt to make a soft dough. Chill the dough; then roll out about one-eighth inch thick and cut in circles. Lay on a buttered sheet, prick over with a fork, and bake in a moderate oven.

A GREAT CAKE

- 1 cup sugar
- 1 cup butter
- 5 eggs
- 1 teaspoon cinnamon
- 1 teaspoon nutmeg
- 1 teaspoon mace
- 2 tablespoons hot water
- White wine
- 2 pounds currants
- 4 cups flour
- 1/2 teaspoon soda
- 1/2 teaspoon salt

Cream butter well and add sugar gradually. Add the eggs, well beaten, and spices. Gradually stir in flour, sifted with soda and salt, hot water, and enough white wine to make a stiff dough. Add currants, which have been rolled in flour. Turn into deep pans and bake in a slow oven about three hours. A better result is obtained if the cake pans are set in pans containing a little water during the first half of the baking.

ANOTHER GREAT CAKE

- 3/4 cup butter
- 1 1/2 cups sugar
- 3 eggs
- 1 cup sour cream
- 1 teaspoon soda
- Grated rinds of 2 lemons
- Juice of 1 lemon
- 1/2 teaspoon mace
- 1/2 teaspoon nutmeg
- 1 teaspoon cinnamon
- 1/2 teaspoon salt
- 1/2 pound raisins
- 1/2 pound currants
- 1/4 pound citron
- 3 1/2 cups flour

Cream the butter until light, add the sugar gradually and the well-beaten egg yolks. Dissolve soda in the cream and add to the mixture. Add lemon juice and rind and the flour, sifted with the salt and spices. Stir in the currants, raisins, and citron, which has been cut in thin slices-all well dredged with flour. Finally fold in the beaten egg whites. Bake in a slow oven about two hours.

A GREAT CAKE, ANOTHER WAY

1 quart flour	1 cup heavy cream
2 pounds currants	4 eggs
3/4 pound butter	1 teaspoon cinnamon
1 cup sugar	1 teaspoon nutmeg
1/2 teaspoon salt	1 teaspoon mace
3 tablespoons rose water	1 teaspoon cloves
	1 teaspoon soda

Sift the flour together with the salt and soda. Work the butter into it with the finger tips. Add the sugar, spices, rose water, eggs, and cream. A little more cream may be added, if needed, to form a very stiff dough. Place in deep pans and bake in a slow oven about three hours.

A GREAT CAKE, STILL ANOTHER WAY

1 quart flour	2 tablespoons caraway seeds
1 cup sugar	1/2 teaspoon salt
1 nutmeg, grated	3/4 pound butter
1 teaspoon cloves	1 cup lukewarm water
1 teaspoon mace	6 eggs
1 teaspoon cinnamon	2 pounds currants
1 teaspoon soda	

Sift together flour, soda, salt, and spices. Add sugar, currants, and caraway seeds. Work in the butter and moisten with the eggs and water. Knead well. Bake in two deep pans in a slow oven.

AN EXCELLENT CAKE

- 1 cup sugar
- 1 1/2 cups butter
- 5 eggs
- 1 teaspoon cinnamon
- 1 teaspoon cloves
- 1 teaspoon mace
- 1/2 teaspoon salt
- 1 teaspoon soda
- 2 ounces orange peel, cut fine
- 2 ounces lemon peel, cut fine
- 2 ounces citron, cut fine
- 1 1/2 pounds currants
- 1 cup cream
- 4 cups flour

Cream the butter well. Add sugar, well-beaten eggs, and cream. Sift the flour together with the soda, salt, and spices, and stir into the first mixture. Finally add the fruits, which have been dusted with flour. Bake in a slow oven.

MARCHPANE CAKES

- 1 pound almonds
- 1 pound sugar
- Rose water
- Sugar

For a good marchpane, the almonds should be beaten in a marble mortar, with a spoonful or two of rose water, until very fine. Add the sugar gradually while beating. It will form a thick paste. You may use a food chopper, but the result will never be the same. Dust a board with powdered sugar and roll the paste about a quarter of an inch thick. Cut in fancy shapes. Put on baking sheets covered with white paper and dusted with powdered sugar. Set in a very cool oven for about half an hour or forty minutes to dry out. They may be iced with powdered sugar mixed with rose water to form a thin icing.

LITTLE CAKES

- 3/4 cup sugar
- 3/4 cup butter
- 4 cups flour
- Whites of 10 eggs
- 1 pound currants
- 1 teaspoon grated nutmeg
- Rose water
- Cream
- 1/2 teaspoon salt
- Powdered sugar

Cream together the butter and sugar. Fold in ten well-beaten egg whites, rose water, and the flour, sifted twice with the salt. Add enough heavy cream to make a stiff paste. Beat the paste fifteen minutes with a rolling pin. Roll out and cut into rounds. On each round lay some currants and sprinkle with sugar, nutmeg, and a little rose water. Place another round of paste on this and press the edges together with a fork. Bake in a moderate oven. The cakes may be made any size you please. Brush over with an icing made of the white of an egg beaten with a teaspoon of rose water and enough powdered sugar to spread.

ALMOND CAKES

- 1 cup sugar
- 4 eggs
- 1/4 pound blanched almonds
- 1 cup flour
- 2 tablespoons rose water
- 1/8 teaspoon salt

Beat the eggs until very light. Add the sugar gradually while continuing beating. Put the almonds through a food chopper (Martha Washington pounded hers in a mortar) and mix with two tablespoons of rose water. Stir with the egg mixture. Add flour, sifted together with the salt, and drop by spoonfuls on a buttered sheet. "Let them have an indifferent quick fire."

BISCUIT[1]

- 4 cups flour
- 2 cups sugar
- Yolks of 8 eggs
- Whites of 4 eggs
- 1/4 teaspoon salt
- 1 tablespoon aniseed
- 1 tablespoon caraway or coriander seeds
- 4 tablespoons rose water

Sift together the flour, sugar, and salt. Add the seeds and moisten with the eggs, well-beaten and mixed with the rose water. Knead and beat with a rolling pin until blisters appear. Roll out about one-eighth inch thick, cut into rounds, and set on baking sheets dusted with

[1] "Biskett," as used by Martha Washington, is not what is known as "biscuit" in America today. Bisketts were thin, flat cakes, rather hard, with no leavening agent. They might or might not contain sugar. The Virginia beaten biscuit is somewhat like the ancient biskett.

sugar and flour. Bake in a moderate oven.

BISCUIT, ANOTHER WAY

- 4 cups flour
- 2 cups sugar
- 6 eggs
- 6 tablespoons rose water
- 1/2 teaspoon salt
- 1 tablespoon aniseed
- 2 tablespoons wine

Beat the eggs until light. Add sugar, rose water, and wine gradually. Sift the salt with the flour and add to first mixture, along with the aniseed. Beat well. Form into cakes and bake as in preceding recipe.

CINNAMON BISCUIT

- 4 cups flour
- 1 teaspoon cinnamon
- 1/2 teaspoon salt
- 1 teaspoon aniseed
- 3 eggs
- 1 teaspoon coriander seeds
- 2 teaspoons baking powder
- Warm water

Sift together flour, salt, spices, and baking powder. Add anise and coriander seeds. Add well-beaten eggs and enough warm water to make a stiff paste. Knead well and form into a long roll. Bake in a slow oven three-quarters of an hour. When a day old, cut in slices, butter, sprinkle with sugar and cinnamon, and set in the oven a few minutes before serving.

GINGERBREAD ROYAL

- 2 cups blanched almonds
- Rose water
- 2 cups sifted powdered sugar
- 1/2 teaspoon cinnamon
- 1 tablespoon candied ginger
- 1/2 cup chopped dates
- 1/2 cup raisins

Beat the almonds in a mortar (they may be put through a food chopper) and mix with two tablespoons rose water as they are prepared. Stir in the spices, sugar, and fruit, using enough additional rose water to form a very stiff paste. Roll out on a board dusted with powdered sugar and cut into fancy shapes. Set in a cool oven to dry out.

EXCELLENT FRENCH WAFERS[1]

- 1 cup cream
- 1/8 cup yolks of eggs
- 2 whole eggs
- 1/4 pound butter
- 1/2 teaspoon salt
- 1/4 cup sugar
- 1/4 teaspoon nutmeg
- 1/4 teaspoon mace
- 1 teaspoon cinnamon
- 1 tablespoon rose water
- 1 yeast cake
- 4 to 4 1/2 cups flour

Scald the cream, add sugar, salt, rose water and butter, let stand until cool. Add well-beaten eggs and yolks of eggs, the yeast dissolved in a little warm water, and half the flour, mixed with the spices. Beat well, cover, and set in a warm place to rise until light. Add remaining flour, beat well, and let rise again. Form into

[1] A wafer, according to Webster's New International Dictionary, was "a thin cake or biscuit, apparently formerly identical with or similar to the modern waffle."

what shape you please, let rise once more, and bake in a moderate oven. Martha Washington baked hers in pans known as "tongues."

CRACKNELLS

1 cup sugar
1 cup butter
6 eggs
2 ounces caraway seeds
1/2 cup rose water
1/2 cup orange flower water
4 cups flour
1 teaspoon baking powder
1/4 teaspoon salt

Cream the butter until very light. Add the sugar gradually and well-beaten eggs. Stir in the flour, mixed with the salt and baking powder. Add the caraway seeds before the dough becomes stiff. Strew sugar on heavy white paper and drop the cakes on it, about the size of a walnut. Bake in a medium oven.

CHEESE CAKES WITHOUT CHEESE CURD

2 cups cream
7 eggs
4 tablespoons sugar
1/3 cup fine bread crumbs
1/8 teaspoon cinnamon
1/8 teaspoon nutmeg
1/8 teaspoon salt
2 tablespoons rose water
1/2 cup currants
Pastry

Scald the cream. Stir in slowly the eggs beaten together with the sugar, spices, and bread crumbs. Cook until mixture thickens. Add rose water and currants. Line a dish with pastry and pour the mixture in. Bake until set.

CHEESE CAKES

- 2 cups cottage cheese
- 6 eggs
- 1 cup currants
- 3/4 cup sugar
- 2 tablespoons rose water
- 1/8 teaspoon cinnamon
- 1/8 teaspoon nutmeg
- 1/8 teaspoon salt
- 2 cups cream
- 3/4 cup fine bread crumbs
- 1/2 cup butter
- Pastry

Beat the eggs very light and add to the cottage cheese, together with the spices, salt, and rose water. Pour the cream on the bread crumbs. Set on fire and cook until it thickens, stirring constantly. Add sugar and butter. Let stand until cool. Add to the first mixture and stir in the currants. Line a deep, round dish with pastry. Fill with the mixture, sprinkle a little sugar and a few currants on top, and bake in a slow oven until set and brown on top.

CHEESE CAKES, ANOTHER WAY

- 2 cups cottage cheese
- 1 cup heavy cream
- 1/2 cup fine bread crumbs
- 3/4 cup sugar
- 1/8 teaspoon cinnamon
- 1/8 teaspoon nutmeg
- 1/8 teaspoon salt
- 1/2 cup currants
- 2 tablespoons white wine
- 4 eggs
- Puff paste

Rub the cottage cheese through a fine sieve. Add sugar, spices, wine, bread crumbs, and currants. Beat eggs until light and add. Whip the cream and fold in. Line a deep dish with puff paste. Turn the mixture into it, and bake until set in a moderate oven.

CREAMS AND JELLIES

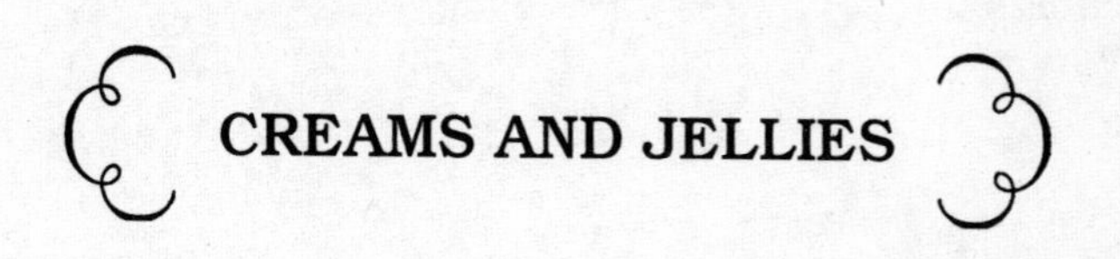

WASHINGTON'S HOME IN NEW YORK

CREAMS AND JELLIES

The sweets served at Mount Vernon were not so different from those of the present. There were, of course, tarts in great variety. Next in choice, perhaps, came the syllabubs, the "Quacking," or "Quakeing," puddings, depending on the author's proclivities in spelling. Blanc Mange, the various "Creams," the "Fools"–whether of orange, lemon, or gooseberry–and the "Trifles," not to forget a "tansey"–a sort of bread pudding made of cream, eggs, Naples biscuit, and currants; flavored with cinnamon, nutmeg, ginger, and tansey, and colored according to the taste of the artist.

A "Syllabub under the Cow" was highly esteemed, although it must have involved a trip to the barnyard. "Put a bottle of either red or white wine, ale or cyder into a china bowl. Sweeten it with sugar and grate in some nutmeg, then hold it under the cow and milk into it till it has a fine froth at the top; strew over it a handful of currants, clean washed and picked and plumped before the fire."

Jellies in a great variety were much favored. Here Mrs. Washington was free to exercise her most romantic fancy in color, shape, and flavor. Although colors were not to be conveniently had in pellets or bottles, she was not dismayed. Spinach was used to produce a green jelly, saffron for a yellow, the juice of beet roots baked in wine produced a beautiful red, and syrup of violets was to be had for purple. As early as 1730 there appeared a recipe for "Ribband or Checker'd Jelly," of which the author is enormously proud. We may look askance at "Gold Fish in Jelly" or "Hen's Nest in Jelly," but in the Washingtons' time they were the pride of the table.

"Gold Fish in Jelly" was indeed a dish for an extraordinary occasion. To make it, you "fill two or three small fish moulds with very strong blanc' mange, when cold turn them out and gild the fish with leaf-gold, let stand for one hour that the gold may dry on. Have a mould. Put a little mould jelly at the bottom, when it is cold lay gold fish in back downwards, put in some jelly bloodwarm to fasten them in their places. When it is cold fill the mould up with blood-warm jelly. The next day turn them all out into a dish and garnish with flowers or anything you fancy."

Our favorite American sweet, ice cream, does not appear in Martha Washington's cook book, which is not surprising in view of when the book was written. The first recipe for ice cream to appear in print in America is in a cook book published in Philadelphia in 1792. Thomas Jefferson became familiar with this delicacy in France and brought back a recipe in 1789. Washington, however had already noted in May, 1784, that he spent "1. 13. 4 by a cream Machine for Ice." Exactly how the Washington ice cream was made, we do not know, but doubtless much after the recipe printed in 1792. The process recommended was similar to that employed in the vacuum freezer today. A pewter basin, containing a mixture of cream, eggs, and sugar, was set within a larger one and surrounded by ice. The contents were stirred at frequent intervals, and "you must prepare it in a part of the house where as little of the warm air comes as you can possibly contrive."

A FINE CREAM

- 4 cups heavy cream
- 6 tablespoons white wine
- 4 tablespoons rose water
- 6 tablespoons sugar
- Few grains of salt

Mix the ingredients in the order given. Let stand for two hours. Beat with an egg beater until it curdles. Turn into a glass dish and let stand half an hour longer before serving.

A WHIPPED POSSET[1]

- 1 quart heavy cream
- 1 pint Rhine wine
- 1 cup white wine
- 1 cup sugar
- Sprig of rosemary
- Piece of lemon peel

Mix the ingredients together in an earthenware bowl. Whip vigorously with a wire whisk. As the froth rises, remove with a silver spoon to sherbet glasses. Serve very cold.

[1] A "posset" was a sort of drink usually made of hot milk and sugar, and curdled with wine or some other liquor. Spices and flavoring were added to taste.

CREAM OF FRENCH BARLEY

1/3 cup pearl barley	3 blades of mace
1 quart cream	Sugar
1 whole nutmeg	Yolks of 3 eggs
1/8 teaspoon salt	1 tablespoon rose water

Wash the barley well and cook in boiling water until tender. Drain. Scald the cream together with the nutmeg, cut in quarters, mace, and salt. Add the barley and boil for fifteen minutes. Beat eggs well, add sugar to taste and rose water. Stir mixture carefully into the cream, being sure it does not curdle. Pour into a glass dish and serve cold.

A SYLLABUB[1]

1 quart cream	6 tablespoons sugar
1 cup white wine	1 whole nutmeg
2 tablespoons rose water	Rind of 1/2 lemon
Sprig of rosemary	Salt

Scald the cream together with the nutmeg, cut in quarters. Remove from fire and, when cool, pour in a glass jar. Let stand overnight. Mix the white wine, rose water, sugar, and pinch of salt. Pour the cream over this and lay in the rosemary and lemon peel. Let stand for five or six hours, until curds form.

[1] A "syllabub" was a favorite delicacy from the sixteenth century to the middle of the nineteenth. It was usually made by combining wine, cider, or some other acid substance with milk or cream, sugar, and other flavoring, and letting this mixture stand until it curdled. Sometimes a syllabub was made of heavy cream mixed with wine and sugar, and beaten to a froth. This was known as a "whipt syllabub."

CREAM WITH CURDS

- 1 pint cream
- Whites of 2 eggs
- Yolks of 4 eggs
- 3 tablespoons sugar
- 1/2 whole nutmeg
- Blade of mace
- 1/8 teaspoon salt

Put the cream, together with the mace and nutmeg, in a double boiler and boil for fifteen minutes. Beat the eggs with the sugar and salt, and add to the cream. Continue cooking and stirring until mixture curdles. Lay a piece of fine cheesecloth in a strainer and pour the custard into this. Let it stand about fifteen minutes. Break the curds up fine, place in a glass or china bowl, and sprinkle with a little sugar. When ready to serve, pour the whey around it. It may be served with cream or white wine instead.

SNOW CREAM

- 4 cups cream
- Whites of 6 eggs
- 6 tablespoons sugar
- 3 tablespoons rose water
- 6 whole cloves
- Piece of stick cinnamon
- 1/2 whole nutmeg
- Yolks of 4 eggs
- Pinch of salt

Mix together the cream, sugar, rose water, salt, and unbeaten egg whites. Beat mixture with an egg beater, and as the foam rises, skim it off with a large spoon and set to drain in a strainer. When as many of these "islands" have been prepared as are desired, place remaining cream in double boiler, together with the spices, and scald. Add egg yolks slightly beaten and stir until thick. Strain into a glass dish. When cold, cover with the "snow."

RASPBERRY CREAM

2 cups cream
Whites of 3 eggs
Blade of mace
Rind of 1/2 lemon
3 tablespoons sugar
Salt
2/3 cup raspberry juice

Beat the egg whites and add to the cream together with sugar, pinch of salt, mace, and lemon rind. Bring to a boil, stirring constantly. Remove from the fire, add raspberry juice, and turn into a glass serving dish. When cool, set in the refrigerator for several hours. Currant and lemon cream may be made the same way.

APPLE CREAM

2 cups sour apple sauce
2 tablespoons rose water
2 cups heavy cream
Sugar

Sweeten the apple sauce to taste and stir the rose water into it. Beat the cream until stiff and fold into the apple sauce. Set in refrigerator for an hour and serve very cold.

GOOSEBERRY CREAM

1 quart gooseberries
2 cups sugar
2 cups heavy cream
2 tablespoons rose water
1/3 cup water

Wash and pick over the gooseberries. Put them in a pan with the sugar and water, and cook slowly about forty minutes. Let cool and press through a sieve. Whip the cream, add rose water, and fold into the fruit. Turn into a glass dish. Serve very cold.

TO MAKE A FOOL

2 cups cream	1 tablespoon rose water
Mace	Salt
Yolks of 4 eggs	Triangles of cake or bread
3 tablespoons sugar	

Candied lemon peel or citron

Scald the cream together with a few grains of mace. Beat the yolks of the eggs with the sugar, salt, and rose water, and stir into the cream. Cook, stirring constantly until mixture thickens. Dip small triangles of cake or bread in cream and line the bottom of a glass dish with them. Pour the custard over them and let stand overnight. Before serving, dust with sugar and decorate with fancy pieces of candied lemon peel or citron.

WHITE LEACH[1]

1 pint cream	Salt
1/2 pound almonds	3 to 4 tablespoons sugar
6 tablespoons rose water	
Blade of mace	1 tablespoon gelatine

2 tablespoons water

Shell and blanch the almonds. Pound to a paste in a mortar, adding the rose water gradually. Combine this with the cream, mace, sugar, and a pinch of salt. Bring to a boil. Soak the gelatine for five minutes in water. Dissolve in the scalding cream. Strain through a fine strainer into a mould. It was usual to eat this with wine or cream as a sauce.

[1] "White Leach" was a sort of jelly usually made with cream and almonds and, in the old days, isinglass instead of gelatine. It was served as a dessert.

A CUSTARD

2 cups cream	3 tablespoons sugar
Yolks of 4 eggs	1/8 teaspoon grated nutmeg
White of 1 egg	2 tablespoons rose water
Salt	

Beat the yolks and whites of eggs together slightly. Add sugar, pinch of salt, and grated nutmeg. Slowly add the cream, stirring well. Flavor with rose water. Pour into custard cups. Set in a pan of water and bake in a very moderate oven until set.

APPLES WITH CREAM

2 cups apple sauce	2 tablespoons rose water
2 cups thick cream	3 tablespoons sugar

The apple sauce should be thick, made of sour apples, and sweetened to taste. Put it in a glass dish. Add sugar and rose water to the cream and set mixture on the fire to boil. Let it boil briskly, and as the foam rises, remove it with a silver spoon and place on top of the apples until the dish is full. Cool any remaining cream and serve as a sauce. All should be very cold.

PUDDINGS

GARDEN LANE, MOUNT VERNON

PUDDINGS

The Mount Vernon puddings were largely of the sturdy English variety, boiled or baked, as the case might be, redolent with spices, and plump with "currans" or "raisins of ye sun." Almonds, cottage cheese, bread and bread crumbs, wine, and rose water were frequently employed.

"Hasty pudding" was a favorite dish of the period, eaten in nearly every colonial home. Although Martha Washington's cook book does not include a recipe for it, it doubtless appeared upon her table. An old magazine gives amusing directions as to the proper manner of eating one. "The hasty-pudding being spread out equally on a plate, while hot, an *excavation* is made in the middle of it with a *spoon*, into which *excavation* a piece of butter as large as a nutmeg is put, and upon it a spoonful of brown sugar, etc. The butter, being soon heated by the heat of the pudding, mixes with the sugar and forms a sauce, which, *being confined in the excavation,* occupies *the middle of the plate!*

"Thus for the array–now for the battle! Dip each *spoonful* in the *sauce, before it is carried to the mouth,* care being had in taking it up to begin on the outside and near the brim of the plate, and to approach the centre by gradual advances, in order not to demolish too soon the *excavation* which forms the reservoir of *sauce.*"

BOILED ALMOND PUDDING

1	pint cream	2	blades of mace
1/4	pound almonds	1/4	whole nutmeg
2	tablespoons rose water	5	eggs
1	tablespoon flour	1/4	cup sugar

Salt

Blanch the almonds and put through the finest food chopper. Turn into a mortar and pound, together with the rose water. Scald the cream with the mace and nutmeg. Beat the eggs; mix together flour, sugar, and a pinch of salt, and stir into the eggs. Add the almond mixture to the cream, and when at the boiling point, stir in carefully the egg mixture. Cook until the spoon is coated. Strain into a glass dish.

BAKED ALMOND PUDDING

1/2 pound almonds
1 pint cream
Yolks of 5 eggs
Whites of 2 eggs
3 tablespoons rose water
Sugar
Salt
Marrow, or butter
Puff paste

Blanch the almonds (they are weighed without shells) and put through the finest food chopper. Turn into a mortar and pound with a pestle, adding the rose water. Beat the egg yolks and whites; add salt and sugar to taste, and then the almond paste. Put all through a strainer. Line a dish with ordinary pastry. Pour into it the almond mixture, dot with bits of marrow or butter, cover with puff paste, and bake in a moderate oven until set.

A MADE DISH

8 slices of white bread
White wine
Yolks of 3 eggs
3/4 cup cream
Sugar
Grated nutmeg
Butter

Cover the sliced bread with the wine and let soak overnight. Beat the egg yolks with the cream and sugar. Drain the bread carefully from the wine and lay in the second mixture, turning so that both sides are coated. Melt some butter in a frying pan and fry the bread until a golden brown on both sides. Arrange on a platter, "strew on it sugar and grated nutmeg and soe serve it up."

A TANSY

- 1 cup fine bread crumbs
- 2 cups cream
- 1/3 cup sugar
- 1/8 teaspoon salt
- 4 eggs
- 1/4 cup melted butter
- 1/2 teaspoon grated nutmeg
- 3 tablespoons rose water
- Green coloring
- Orange juice
- Orange slices

Soak the bread crumbs in the cream until soft. Add sugar, salt, melted butter, rose water, and nutmeg. Color to suit taste with green coloring paste. Lastly add the well-beaten eggs. Turn into a buttered dish and bake until set. When done, sprinkle with orange juice and sugar, and decorate with triangles of sliced orange.

Martha Washington used bruised spinach and sorrel to color her tansy, but the modern artificial coloring serves just as well. She also used a handful of tansy leaves, crushed, to impart their bitter flavor. As tansy is almost unobtainable now, it may perforce be omitted.

APPLE TANSY

- Whites of 6 eggs
- Yolks of 3 eggs
- 2 tablespoons rose water
- Juice 1/2 lemon
- 1/8 teaspoon salt
- 1/8 teaspoon grated nutmeg
- 2 tablespoons sugar
- 6 apples
- 2 tablespoons butter

Beat the eggs well. Add rose water, lemon juice, sugar, salt, and nutmeg. Peel and core four apples and cut up in very fine pieces. Add to the first mixture. Peel the remaining two apples, cut crosswise in thin slices, and fry in butter until brown. Set in a place to keep warm. Now melt the butter in a skillet and pour in the apple and egg mixture; it should be fairly thick. With a silver spoon, pat it down to form a round cake. Let it cook slowly until brown on one side; then turn and brown on the other side. It may be necessary to add more butter. Turn onto a warm platter and place the fried apple circles on top. Sprinkle with sugar and a little rose water. Serve hot.

A LIGHT PUDDING

1 cup bread
2 cups milk
6 eggs
1/3 cup sugar
2 tablespoons rose water
Grated nutmeg
Salt
Almonds

Take several slices of bread, remove crust, and break into small pieces; there should be one cupful. Pour onto it the milk, set on a low fire, and boil until thick. Beat with a spoon until the mixture forms a smooth mass. Add sugar, rose water, pinch of salt, dash of nutmeg, and well-beaten eggs. Butter a baking dish and turn the pudding into it. Set in a pan of water and bake forty-five minutes in a slow oven. Remove from oven and decorate with blanched almonds.

SAUCE FOR A LIGHT PUDDING

1/3 cup butter
1 cup powdered sugar
1 tablespoon rose water

Cream the butter until very light. Add sugar gradually, drop by drop, so as not to curdle. Add rose water. Turn into serving dish and grate nutmeg over the top.

A GOOD PUDDING

1 cup bread crumbs	Grated nutmeg
2 cups cream	2 tablespoons rose water
4 eggs	1/3 cup sugar
1/4 pound beef suet	1/8 teaspoon salt
1/2 cup currants	

Scald the cream and add bread crumbs slowly. Beat well. Add the suet, ground very fine, sugar, salt, nutmeg, rose water, and well-beaten eggs. "Put in or leave out currants at your pleasure." Turn into a buttered baking dish and bake in a slow oven for forty minutes. Serve with the following sauce.

SAUCE FOR A GOOD PUDDING

1/3 cup butter	1 cup powdered sugar
1 teaspoon vinegar	

Cream the butter well, adding the sugar gradually. When very light add the vinegar, drop by drop.

STEWED PUDDINGS

1 pound clear veal	1 1/2 cups currants
1 cup bread crumbs	3/4 pound suet
3 eggs	1 nutmeg, grated
1 cup sugar	1/2 teaspoon salt
1/2 cup flour	

Grind the veal and suet. Mix together with bread crumbs, sugar, spices, flour, and currants. Beat the eggs and add to other ingredients. Form into balls and poach in broth or hot water about forty minutes. Drain and serve hot with sugar and butter creamed together and flavored with lemon.

A CURD PUDDING

2 cups cottage cheese
1/4 cup suet
1/8 teaspoon nutmeg
2 tablespoons flour
2 tablespoons rose water
1/4 teaspoon salt
4 eggs
2/3 cup currants
Powdered sugar

Grind the suet very fine. Add it to the cheese, together with the sugar, flour, spices, and rose water. Beat well. Beat eggs until light and add. Dust the currants with flour and stir them in. Turn into a baking dish and bake in a slow oven until set. Dust with powdered sugar before serving.

A MADE DISH OF GOOSEBERRIES

1 pint gooseberries
1/2 cup water
1 1/2 to 2 cups sugar
Yolks of 6 eggs
3 tablespoons rose water

Pick over the gooseberries and remove, the sharp points. Add the water and cook to a pulp. Add the sugar as required and stir well. Beat the egg yolks together with the rose water and add to the gooseberry mixture. Let it boil up for a moment or two, stirring constantly. Serve in a silver dish. "It is good eyther hot or cold but it is best cold."

A QUAKEING PUDDING

- 1 quart cream
- 3 tablespoons flour
- 1/2 nutmeg, grated
- 1/2 cup sugar
- 10 eggs
- 1/8 teaspoon salt

Put the flour into a bowl, add five tablespoons of cream, and beat until perfectly smooth. Add the nutmeg, sugar, salt, and eggs, well beaten. Beat for fifteen minutes. Add the remaining cream and stir until thoroughly blended. Moisten a linen napkin and butter it well. Lay napkin in a bowl and pour in the pudding. Gather ends of the napkin and tie up tight. Plunge in boiling water and boil for half an hour.

TO MAKE A MARROW PUDDING

- Dry bread
- Raisins
- Apples
- 2 tablespoons marrow or butter
- Salt
- 3 cups cream
- Yolks of 3 eggs
- 5 tablespoons sugar
- 2 blades mace
- 1/4 whole nutmeg

Scald the cream together with the mace and nutmeg. Beat egg yolks; add sugar and a pinch of salt. Pour into the cream and stir until it thickens. Remove from fire and strain.

Cut the bread in thin slices and remove crusts. Butter a deep pudding dish and lay in it a layer of bread, then a handful of raisins, a layer of apples peeled and cut in thin slices, and small squares of marrow or butter.

On this, pour some of the hot cream mixture. Repeat the bread-, raisin-, apple-, marrow-mixture until the dish is full. Pour the remaining cream and egg mixture over all and bake in a moderate oven about thirty-five minutes, until set and pale brown.

RICE FLORENTINE

- 1/2 cup rice
- 1 cup scalded milk
- 1/8 teaspoon cloves
- 1/8 teaspoon cinnamon
- 1/8 teaspoon nutmeg
- 1/8 teaspoon salt
- 1/2 cup white wine
- 2 tablespoons melted butter
- 2 tablespoons rose water
- 1/2 cup raisins
- 1/2 cup currants
- 4 eggs
- Powdered sugar

Wash rice and cook in boiling salted water until half done. Drain and cover with scalded milk. Cook until this is absorbed and the rice is soft. Season with cinnamon, cloves, nutmeg, and salt. Add white wine, rose water raisins, currants, well-beaten eggs, melted butter, and sugar to taste, about half a cup. Beat well, turn into a pie shell, preferably of puff paste, and bake in a moderate oven until set. Dust with powdered sugar before serving.

AN HERB PUDDING

1	cup oatmeal	1/4	cup currants
4	eggs	2	tablespoons rose water
1/2	teaspoon cinnamon	1/3	cup melted butter
1/2	teaspoon nutmeg	1/4	teaspoon salt
1	teaspoon allspice		Milk
1/2	teaspoon ginger		Sugar

Cover the oatmeal with hot milk and let soak overnight. When ready to make the pudding, stir in the sugar, melted butter, spices, well-beaten eggs, and the currants, dusted with flour. Mix well, turn into a floured cloth, drop in boiling water, and cook gently for an hour and a half. Turn onto a platter, pour melted butter over and around it, and sprinkle with sugar.

A FRIED PUDDING

	Yolks of 4 eggs	1/4	teaspoon nutmeg
	Whites of 2 eggs	1/8	teaspoon salt
3/4	cup cream		Bread crumbs
	Sugar	2	tablespoons flour
1/4	teaspoon cinnamon	1/2	cup currants

Beat the yolks and whites of eggs together until very light. Add the cream and enough bread crumbs to form a medium-stiff dough. Add two tablespoons sugar, salt, spices, flour, and currants. Melt some butter in a large skillet. Pour in the mixture and fry until a golden brown; turn and fry on the other side. Sprinkle with sugar and serve.

A RICE PUDDING

1/4	pound rice	2	tablespoons rose water
3	cups milk	1/2	teaspoon cinnamon
1/4	pound mutton suet		Salt
	Yolks of 6 eggs		Sugar
	Whites of 2 eggs		Currants

Wash the rice and cook in as much milk as it will absorb, about three cups, stirring often with a silver fork. When dry and tender, add the suet, minced very fine, the beaten yolks and whites of eggs, and sugar and salt to taste. Stir in rose water and cinnamon. Lastly add the currants, turn into a baking dish, and bake in a moderate oven until set.

A WHITE PUDDING

3	cups milk	1/2	teaspoon salt
1	quart oatmeal	3	tablespoons rose water
1 1/2	pounds suet	1	cup sugar
1	nutmeg, grated	1/2	cup bread crumbs
	Yolks of 4 eggs	1 1/2	cup currants
	White of 1 egg		

Cream

Scald the milk and add oatmeal. When mixture comes to a boil, cover and let stand all night. Chop the suet very fine and mix with the oatmeal. Add the sugar, well-beaten eggs, bread crumbs, spices, and currants, rolled in flour. If the dough seems too thick, add a little cream. Put in a pudding mould and boil three hours.

TO MAKE A FIRMETY

1 cup milk	1 tablespoon flour
1 cup cream	1/8 teaspoon salt
Yolks of 6 eggs	1/3 cup sugar
Whites of 2 eggs	1/2 cup seedless raisins

Grated nutmeg

Scald the milk and cream together with the nutmeg. Mix the flour, sugar, and salt together. Beat the eggs until very light and gradually beat into them the flour and sugar mixture. Add to the scalding milk and stir, in a double boiler, until thick. Add the raisins, which have been soaked in hot water for half an hour and dried. Turn into a glass dish and serve hot or cold.

CHEESE LOAVES

2 cups curds	1/4 teaspoon grated nutmeg
6 eggs	1/8 teaspoon salt
2/3 cup granulated sugar	1/3 cup melted butter
Bread crumbs	3/4 cup powdered sugar
1/8 teaspoon cloves	

1 tablespoon rose water

Mash the curds fine. Add well-beaten eggs, sugar, spices, and enough fine bread crumbs to enable you to form the mixture into small loaves, about the size of dinner rolls. Place on buttered paper and bake in a moderate oven until firm. Mix powdered sugar with melted butter and rose water. Slit across the top of each little loaf and insert a teaspoonful of this mixture.

VERY GOOD PUDDING CAKES

1 pint cream
3 eggs
3 tablespoons sugar
1/4 teaspoon ginger
1/4 teaspoon grated nutmeg
Cinnamon
1 1/2 cups bread crumbs
1/2 cup flour
1/4 cup marrow or suet
1/2 cup currants
1/8 teaspoon salt
1 tablespoon rose water

Beat the eggs until light. Add the cream, bread crumbs, sugar, spices, rose water, marrow chopped very fine, and currants, which have been dusted with flour. Form into small cakes and fry on each side until golden brown. If necessary, a little more flour may be added. Place on a platter and sprinkle with sugar and cinnamon.

LOAF PUDDING

1 loaf of bread
Milk
Yolks of 4 eggs
Grated nutmeg
1/2 cup currants
1/2 cup raisins
1/4 pound beef suet
3/4 cup sugar
Salt

Take a small, square loaf of bread. Cut off the top and remove the soft part, leaving only the shell. Crumble the bread fine and soak in enough hot milk to moisten well. Add beaten egg yolks, sugar, spices, suet ground very fine, and raisins and currants, dusted with flour. Refill the loaf and put back the cover. Brush over with milk and egg, and bake in a slow oven one hour.

PRESERVES

VEGETABLE GARDEN, MOUNT VERNON

PRESERVES

There were no refrigerator cars to rush strawberries, fresh peas, asparagus, and other delicacies from California or Florida to the table at Mount Vernon; no express liners to bring peaches and lobster from Africa in the dead of winter, or pears from the Argentine. In the abundant summer months these things had to be preserved, and thus it happens that a large section of the *Cook Book*, "A Booke of Sweetmeats," is devoted to the art of preserving and making "marmelets." Cherries, "apricocks," damsons, grapes, gooseberries, peaches, and pippins all found their way to the ample preserving kettle, not to mention quince, for which there are more than a dozen recipes. Rose leaves and rose buds, along with barberries and rosemary flowers, were also not neglected.

Other sweets were not forgotten–there was no confectioner at hand to provide a "sampler"–and many are the recipes for "lozenges," "candied rose leaves" "violet paste," or "marchpane conceits." Most of these have been omitted here, as no woman of this age would have the time or desire to experiment with this long-lost art.

PRESERVED GRAPES

Grapes | Sugar
Water

Take the fairest green grapes as soon as they are ripe, slit them in the side, and carefully remove the seeds. Weigh them, and to each pound of fruit allow one pound of sugar and two tablespoons of water. Set the sugar and water on the fire, bring to a boil, skim, and let cool. Add the grapes. Set mixture on the fire again and let it boil up quickly. When the grapes begin to shrink and the syrup to thicken, remove the fruit and put it in glasses with a very little of the syrup. Boil the remainder to a jelly and pour over the grapes through a strainer.

WHOLE PRESERVED ORANGES AND LEMONS

Oranges | Sugar
Lemons | Water

Take the desired number of oranges and lemons, small ones, and lay them in water overnight. Boil until tender, changing the water several times. When tender, weigh them, and allow one pound of sugar for each pound of fruit. Add enough water to make a syrup which will nearly cover them, and boil the fruit half an hour. Remove the fruit to sterilized jars and boil the syrup until thick; then pour it over the oranges and lemons.

PRESERVED APRICOTS

4 pounds apricots | 3 pounds sugar

Wash the apricots carefully, peel, cut in halves, and remove stones. Place in a preserving kettle and pour the sugar over them, seeing that they are well and carefully mixed. Let stand overnight. In the morning, set on a low fire and bring to a boil. Boil slowly about three-quarters of an hour. Put in sterilized glasses and seal.

PRESERVED CHERRIES

3 pounds cherries | 2 pounds sugar

Wash the cherries. Remove stems and stones from two pounds. Crush the remaining pound and strain the juice through a fine cheesecloth. Add sugar to the juice and bring to a boil. Add the pitted cherries and cook slowly for about three-quarters of an hour, or until the syrup jellies. Pour into sterilized jars or glasses.

PRESERVED GOOSEBERRIES

1 pound gooseberries | 1 pound sugar

Take the fairest berries you can get, remove the prickly end and wash. Put a layer of berries in the bottom of a pan, then a layer of sugar, and so on until all is used up. Add three or four tablespoons of water and set on a low fire. Shake them often until the sugar is melted, then boil briskly until the berries are clear. It takes about forty minutes. Turn into sterilized glasses.

ORANGE MARMALADE

Oranges	Apples
Sugar	Rose water

Lay the desired number of oranges in water for several days. Boil them whole until tender, changing the water twice. Pare them, remove white membrane and put the skins through a food chopper. Boil some apples in very little water until tender and press through a sieve. To one pound of the orange pulp add one pound of apple pulp, one pound of sugar and one-half cup of rose water. Boil until it thickens, about three-quarters of an hour.

PRESERVED PEACHES

2 pounds peaches	2 cups water
1 pint white wine	Sugar

Wipe the peaches off with a clean cloth and parboil them in wine and water, mixed. When tender, remove the skins and weigh them. For each pound of peaches, allow three-quarters of a pound of sugar. Dissolve this in one cup of white wine and boil for half an hour. Add the peaches and let them lie in the syrup for another half hour. Then bring to a boil and cook briskly for ten minutes. Put into sterilized jars.

PRESERVED PLUMS IN JELLY

2 pounds plums	2 pounds sugar
2 cups apple water	

Take two cups of water in which apples have been boiled. Add sugar and stir until dissolved. Add the plums, which have been carefully washed, and boil slowly until tender. Set aside to cool and let stand two days. Remove the plums to sterilized glasses. Bring the syrup to a boil, skim, and let boil ten minutes. Then pour syrup over the plums and seal.

PRESERVED DAMSON PLUMS

2 pounds damson plums
2 pounds sugar
Water

Wash the plums and prick each one with a skewer or the end of a small knife. Put half the sugar in a kettle and add enough water barely to moisten it. Lay the plums on this and cover with remaining sugar. Set on a low fire and boil gently until nearly tender. Increase the heat and boil more rapidly until done. Turn into sterilized glasses. Be sure to choose damsons that are not too ripe; otherwise they will cook to pieces.

TO PRESERVE PIPPINS RED

Pippins
Sugar
Stick cinnamon
Water

Wash and pare the pippins and remove the cores. For each pound of fruit, allow three-quarters of a pound of sugar, three-quarters of a cup of water, and one piece of stick cinnamon. Dissolve the sugar in the water and boil five minutes in a broad-bottomed pan. Add the apples and cinnamon, cover, and let boil gently until the fruit is tender, turning several times. When the apples begin to jelly, remove to glasses and pour the syrup over them. A few drops of red coloring are an improvement.

PRESERVED PIPPINS

Pippins
Lemons
Orange rind
Sugar
Rose water

Wash the pippins and peel very thin. Cut in halves and place in water so that they will not turn dark. For every pound of pippins, allow one pound of sugar and a cup of water and 2 tablespoons of rose water. Mix half the sugar with the water and bring to a boil. Add the pippins and cook slowly for fifteen minutes. Add the remaining sugar, little by little, the juice of a lemon, and the rind of an orange, which has been boiled in two waters and cut in fine slivers. Cook until the apples are thoroughly tender and transparent.

RED MARMALADE OF QUINCES

Quinces
Sugar
Water

Wash the quinces thoroughly; cut in half, remove cores, and peel. Nearly cover them with water and let stand overnight. Save the parings and cores. Drain the quinces, add parings and cores to the water, and boil for an hour. Strain. To every pound of quince, add a pint of this water and a pound of sugar. Boil until the quinces are tender. Crush the quinces as the marmalade cooks in order that it may not be lumpy.

TO PRESERVE QUINCES YELLOW

4 pounds quinces | 4 pounds sugar
Water

Wash, pare, and core the quinces. Boil them in clear water until they are soft. Add three cups of water to the sugar and boil ten minutes, removing any scum. Add the quinces and boil until they are so tender you can pass a straw through them. Take them up and boil the syrup a little thicker by itself. Then combine syrup and fruit, which will look yellow-according to Martha Washington.

TO PRESERVE QUINCES RED

Quinces | Sugar
Water

Take ripe, yellow quinces and core them at the top. Parboil in a kettle of clear water until they are somewhat tender, having first put into the kettle the quince kernels and two or three quinces cut in pieces. When tender, remove the fruit from the kettle; and when cold, pare as thin as you can. Weigh the quinces. To every pound, allow one pound of sugar; and to every pound of sugar, a pint of the water in which the quinces were boiled. Boil the sugar and water for fifteen minutes; then add the quinces and cook gently until the syrup begins to thicken. Keep well covered and let fruit boil until it is red in color and the syrup will jell. Shake the pot once in a while and remove the scum. Put each quince in a little pot or glass and pour some of the jelly over it. A little red coloring paste has been known to help.

RASPBERRY MARMALADE

1 pound raspberries
1/2 pound sugar
2 tablespoons rose water

Wash the raspberries carefully. Dissolve the sugar in the rose water and boil for five minutes. Crush the raspberries and add, stirring well. Cook slowly until thick, about forty minutes. Turn into sterilized glasses.

WHITE QUINCE MARMALADE

Quinces
Sugar

Wash, pare, core, and quarter the quinces. As fast as this is done, cover them with sugar and let stand for three hours. For every pound of quinces, allow three-quarters of a pound of sugar. Set on a low fire until the sugar starts melting; then boil rapidly for half to three-quarters of an hour. Break the quinces in pieces with a fork or spoon as they become tender.

QUIDONY[1] OF QUINCE

2 pounds quinces
1 pound sugar
1 quart water

Wash, pare, and cut the quinces in pieces. Put into a pot with the water. Boil until tender; then wring the liquor from them through a cheesecloth. Put juice into a clean pan with the sugar and let it boil until it begins to turn dark and forms a thick jelly. Pour it into moulds that have been rinsed in cold water.

[1] A thick jelly or paste.

A MARMALADE THAT WAS PRESENTED TO THE QUEEN FOR A NEW YEAR'S GIFT

1 1/2 pounds, sugar
6 quinces
4 ounces candied orange peel
3 ounces of blanched almonds
2 tablespoons rose water
Piece of stick cinnamon
10 whole cloves
Blade of mace
6 pieces of candied ginger

Dissolve the sugar in a pint of water and cook for ten minutes. Wash, core, and pare the quinces, cut in small pieces, and put in the syrup. Cook until nearly tender. Add the almonds, cut in fine slivers, rose water, spices, and orange peel and ginger, cut very fine. Cook mixture until thick, about half an hour longer. "This being done, box it up and present it to whom you please."

PRESERVED RED ROSE LEAVES

Red rose leaves
1 pint water
1 pound sugar

Take half a pound of the finest red rose buds and sift them clear of their seeds. Put a pint of water in a pan on the stove, and when it boils, add a handful of other red rose leaves and simmer until they begin to lose their color. Repeat this several times until the water is very red. Then add sugar and boil ten minutes. Add the half pound of selected rose leaves and boil slowly for about three-quarters of an hour. Turn into sterilized glasses.

PRESERVED RASPBERRIES

1 pound raspberries — 1 pound sugar
1 cup currant juice

Carefully wash the raspberries, put in a pan, and strew the sugar on them. Let stand for two or three hours. Set on the stove and bring to a boil. Add the currant juice and boil rapidly until the berries are tender. Remove fruit to glasses. Boil the juice ten minutes longer and pour over the berries.

QUIDONY OF RASPBERRIES AND RED ROSES

1 pound raspberries — 1/4 pound red rose leaves
Sugar

Put the raspberries and rose leaves in a dish and crush thoroughly with the back of a silver spoon. Wring the juice from them through a piece of cheesecloth. Add an equal amount of sugar and set on a slow fire. Boil until it thickens, about half an hour. Pour into small glasses.

A MARMALADE THAT WILL KEEP TWO OR THREE YEARS

Quinces — Sugar

Take the best apple quinces obtainable, wash well, and lay them in a pan so that they barely touch. Set them in a moderate oven and bake until tender. Then remove the skins, scrape the pulp from them, not taking too much from the core, and allow the full weight in sugar. Boil the pap and the sugar together until it stiffens slightly when tried on a cold saucer. Then put in glasses which have been sterilized.

CANDIED GOOSEBERRIES

Gooseberries Sugar
Rose water

Take green gooseberries, wash well, and remove stem and blossom ends. Dry them on a piece of linen. For every ounce of berries, allow two ounces of sugar and one ounce of rose water. Boil the sugar and rose water until it will spin a light thread. Set in a pan of cold water, to stop the boiling. Cool a few moments. Add the berries and stir until all are coated. Turn on oiled paper and set in a cool oven.

TO STEW WARDENS[1]

Wash and peel the pears, leaving them whole, with the stems on. Make a syrup of 1 cup of sugar and 1/2 cup of water. Let cook five minutes. Add pears, two or three pieces of stick cinnamon, and 1/4 cup rose water. Stew slowly until tender.

The pears may be cut in quarters and cored before stewing. In this case they may be put in a pie shell with criss-cross strips of pastry and baked.

[1] A variety of winter pear.

CANDIED VIOLET LEAVES

In the spring, when the fields are a carpet of violets and you feel very gay, try this recipe.

"To every ounce of violets," says Martha Washington, "take 4 ounces of sugar and dissolve it in 2 ounces of water. Soe boyl it till it turn to sugar againe, and scum it very often that it may be very clear." Remove from the fire, cool slightly, add the violets and stir until well coated. Turn on a white paper and set in a cool oven to dry.

HONEY OF ROSES

1 pint honey	1 pint red rose leaves

Bring the honey to a boil and remove any scum. Add the rose leaves. Set the pan in another pan of hot water and boil for half an hour. More rose leaves may be added after fifteen minutes, if available. Let stand for ten minutes. Strain, while hot, into sterilized jars.

BEVERAGES

BEVERAGES

An important part of the *cuisine* of every colonial establishment was the making of cordial waters and cooling drinks, as they were called. They took the place of the ubiquitous Coca-Cola of the present time. Although a gentleman might take a few mint juleps before breakfast, a bracer in the middle of the morning, a toddy or two before lunch, and a stiffener in the middle of the hot afternoon, the ladies of the household had recourse to a gentle syrup of violets or, at most, to a sip of "parfait d'amour." Almost every fruit and flower was used for this purpose, from raspberries and "leamons" to damask roses and "Mayden Hairs." There was "Sirrup of Purslane," "Sirrup of Horehound," syrup of mulberries, damask roses with rhubarb, of pippins, vinegar, or what you will. Wine was not forgotten, and we find recipes for cherry, blackberry, elderberry, currant, raspberry, and birch wines. Medicinal waters of cinnamon, wormwood, and black cherry were also provided for hard days, along with spirits of mint, saffron, and rosemary flowers. The mistress of Mount

Vernon became something of an alchemist as she faithfully compounded "A very sweet Perfume," a "Perfume to stand in a Roome," "Perfume Powder for Hayre," and even a powder "to keep ye teeth clean and white and to fasten them."

BLACKBERRY WINE

4 quarts blackberries
5 quarts water
1 pound raisins
1 pound loaf sugar
2 lemons, sliced

Crush the berries thoroughly and strain the juice through a fine cloth. Put the raisins through a food chopper; add to the water, together with the lemons, and boil for twenty minutes. Strain this and mix with the fruit juice. Let stand two days. Then add the sugar and strain once more. Bottle and cork.

CHERRY WINE

3 quarts cherry juice
2 pounds raisins
6 quarts boiling water

Put the raisins through a food chopper. Then lay them in a stone jar. Add water, cherry juice, and crushed cherries, from which the juice has been extracted. Cover closely and let stand three days. Strain and let stand three more days. Syphon off the clear juice and strain through. a fine cloth. Pour into sterilized bottles and seal.

LEMON WINE

6 lemons	1 pound loaf sugar
6 quarts water	1 pound raisins

Pare and slice the lemons. Put all the pulp and the rind of one lemon in the water, along with the raisins, which have been cut small or put through a food chopper. Place in an earthen jar and let stand two days. Boil mixture for half an hour. Return to jar and let stand eight days. Syphon off the liquid, strain through a fine cloth, and bottle, adding a lump of sugar to every bottle.

TO MAKE SHRUB

1 quart brandy	1 quart white wine
1 quart water	3 lemons

1 pound sugar

Mix the brandy, wine, and water. Cut up and crush the lemons, and add them along with the sugar. Stir mixture well; put in a stone jar and cover tightly. Let stand three days, stirring every day. On the fourth day, strain and bottle.

SYRUP OF LEMONS

Lemons	Sugar

Squeeze the desired number of lemons and strain the juice through a fine cloth. To one pint of juice, add one and a quarter pounds of sugar. Boil mixture to a syrup and bottle.

SYRUP OF RASPBERRIES

1 quart raspberries — 1 pound sugar

Set the raspberries over a low fire and crush them thoroughly. When they come to a boil, remove from stove and strain the juice through a fine cloth. Add the sugar; there should be a pint of juice to a pound of sugar. Stir until well dissolved; then bring to a boil, remove scum, and boil until it forms a light syrup. Pour into glasses or bottles.

SYRUP OF VIOLETS

1 pound violets — 3 pounds sugar
1 pint water

Boil the sugar and water for ten minutes, removing any scum. Crush the violets in a mortar, add to the syrup, and cook until they lose their color. Strain the juice into a glass dish and bottle when cold.

GOOSEBERRY WINE

3 quarts ripe gooseberries — 1/2 pound loaf sugar
2 gallons water

Crush the gooseberries thoroughly and add the water. Mix well and let stand two hours. Pass through a fine sieve. Add the sugar. Pour in a stone jar and cover so that no air can get to it. Make a hole in the cover and stop this with a cork. Let stand for two days; then give it a little air. After two more days, repeat. Let stand ten days, syphon off the clear liquid, strain through a fine cloth, and bottle. Put a lump of sugar in each bottle and cork. "To this you may put, if you please, two quarts of white wine, which will make it more quick and brisk and strong. This is a good way to make wine of raspberries, mulberries, blackberries, peaches or any other fruit."

METHAGLIN

1 quart honey	1/2 ounce ginger
6 quarts water	1/2 yeast cake

Mix the honey and water, add ginger, and boil until the amount is reduced by a third. When cold, put in a jar together with the yeast, which has been dissolved in a little water. Let stand three days. Syphon it off and bottle, putting in each bottle a small piece of lemon, a small piece of stick cinnamon, and two or three raisins. Wait a fortnight before you drink it.

TO MAKE MEAD

4 pounds raisins	1 lemon
1/4 ounce nutmeg	2 1/2 gallons water
1/2 ounce cinnamon	1 quart honey

1/2 cup rose water

Put raisins through a food chopper. Crush the spices and add, together with the lemon, cut in small pieces. Add the water and honey and let stand four days, stirring each day. Syphon off the clear liquid, add rose water, and bottle.

TO MAKE HIPPOCRAS

2	gallons sauterne	4	ounces ginger
1	gallon chablis	1/2	ounce nutmeg
4 1/2	pounds sugar	1/2	ounce coriander seed
6	ounces stick cinnamon	1/4	ounce cloves

1 quart milk

Mix the wines and add spices–which should, of course, not be powdered–and one pound of sugar. Let stand for twenty-four hours. Add remaining sugar and milk. Mix well and strain twice through a fine cloth. Bottle and cork.

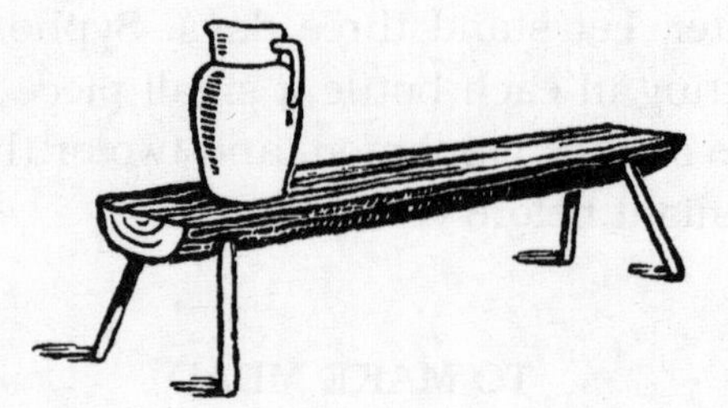

INDEX

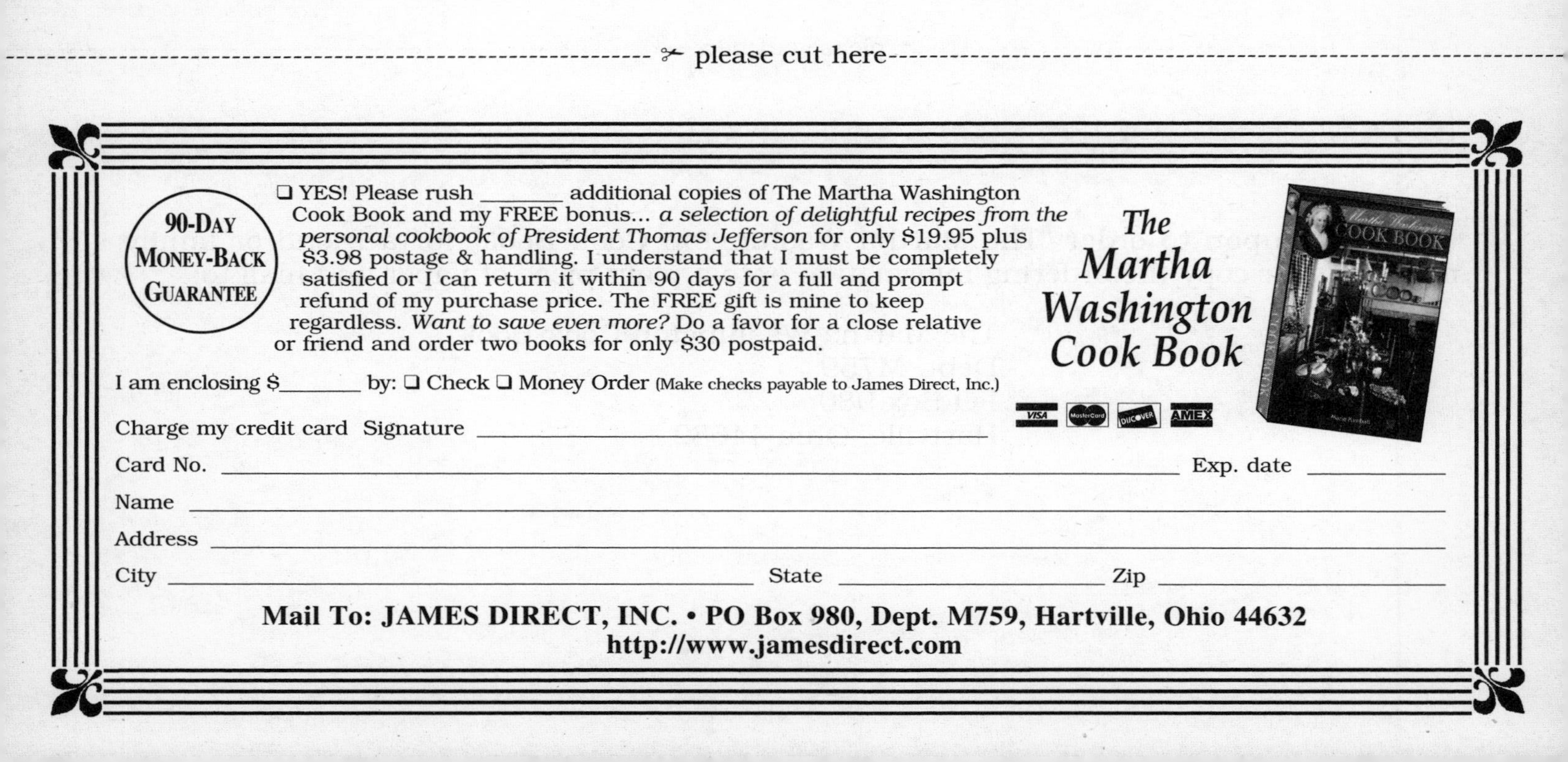
please cut here
90-DAY MONEY-BACK GUARANTEE
❑ YES! Please rush _______ additional copies of The Martha Washington Cook Book and my FREE bonus... a selection of delightful recipes from the personal cookbook of President Thomas Jefferson for only $19.95 plus $3.98 postage & handling. I understand that I must be completely satisfied or I can return it within 90 days for a full and prompt refund of my purchase price. The FREE gift is mine to keep regardless. Want to save even more? Do a favor for a close relative or friend and order two books for only $30 postpaid.
The Martha Washington Cook Book
I am enclosing $_______ by: ❑ Check ❑ Money Order (Make checks payable to James Direct, Inc.)
VISA
MasterCard
DISCOVER
AMEX
Charge my credit card Signature
Card No.
Exp. date
Name
Address
City
State
Zip
Mail To: JAMES DIRECT, INC. • PO Box 980, Dept. M759, Hartville, Ohio 44632
http://www.jamesdirect.com

Preferred Customer Reorder Form

Order this...	If you want a book on...	Cost...	Number of Copies...
Home Remedies from the Old South	Hundreds of little known old-time remedies for aches & pains, cleaning & beauty.	$9.95	
Garlic: Nature's Natural Companion	Exciting scientific research on garlic's ability to promote good health. Find out for yourself why garlic has the reputation of being able to heal almost magically! Newest in Emily's series of natural heath books!	$9.95	
The Vinegar Home Guide	Learn how to clean and freshen with natural, environmentally-safe vinegar in the house, garden and laundry. Plus, delicious home-style recipes!	$9.95	
Amish Gardening Secrets	You too can learn the special gardening secrets the Amish use to produce huge tomato plants and bountiful harvests. Information packed 800-plus collection for you to tinker with and enjoy.	$9.95	
		Total NUMBER of $9.95 items	

Any combination of the above $9.95 items qualifies for the following discounts...

Order any 2 items for: $15.95

Order any 3 items for: $19.95

Order any 4 items for: $24.95

Order any 5 items for: $29.95

Order any 6 items for: $34.95 and receive 7th item FREE

Any additional items for: $5 each

FEATURED SELECTIONS

		Total COST of $9.95 items	
The Vinegar Anniversary Book	Completely updated with the latest research and brand new remedies and uses for apple cider vinegar. Handsome coffee table collector's edition you'll be proud to display. ***Big 208-page book!***	$12.95	
The Magic of Baking Soda	*Plain Old Baking Soda A Drugstore in A Box?* Doctors & researchers have discovered baking soda has amazing healing properties! Over 600 health & Household Hints. *Great Recipes Too!*	$12.95	
The Magic of Hydrogen Peroxide	An Ounce of Hydrogen Peroxide is worth a Pound of Cure! Hundreds of health cures, household uses & home remedy uses for hydrogen peroxide contained in this breakthrough volume.	$19.95	
Thomas Jefferson's Cookbook	Culinary secrets revealed by the Father of Fine Dining in America! Here's a remarkable collection of delightful handwritten recipes – you'll love Jefferson's personal comments in this 128-page book!	$19.95	
The Martha Washington Cookbook	208-page Martha Washington cookbook used at Mount Vernon and later in the Presidential mansion after she became America's first lady. A remarkable collection of delightful handwritten recipes!	$19.95	
Order any 2 or more Featured Selections for only $10 each...		**Postage & Handling**	$3.98*
		TOTAL	

**** Shipping of 10 or more books = $6.96***

90-DAY MONEY-BACK GUARANTEE

Please rush me the items marked above. I understand that I must be completely satisfied or I can return any item within 90 days with proof of purchase for a full and prompt refund of my purchase price.

I am enclosing $_______ by: ❑ Check ❑ Money Order (Make checks payable to James Direct Inc)

VISA MasterCard DISCOVER AMEX

Charge my credit card Signature ____________________

Card No. ____________________ Exp. Date _______

Name ________________ Address ________________

City ________________ State ________________ Zip _______

Telephone Number (_________) ________________

❑ Yes! I'd like to know about freebies, specials and new products before they are nationally advertised. My email address is: ________________

Mail To: **James Direct Inc.** • PO Box 980, Dept. A1235 • Hartville, Ohio 44632
Customer Service (330) 877-0800 • *http://www.jamesdirect.com*